FREE Study Skills Videos

Dear Customer,

Thank you for your purchase from Mometrix! We consider it an honor and a privilege that you have purchased our product and we want to ensure your satisfaction.

As a way of showing our appreciation and to help us better serve you, we have developed Study Skills Videos that we would like to give you for <u>FREE</u>. These videos cover our *best practices* for getting ready for your exam, from how to use our study materials to how to best prepare for the day of the test.

All that we ask is that you email us with feedback that would describe your experience so far with our product. Good, bad, or indifferent, we want to know what you think!

To get your FREE Study Skills Videos, you can use the **QR code** below, or send us an **email** at <u>studyvideos@mometrix.com</u> with *FREE VIDEOS* in the subject line and the following information in the body of the email:

- The name of the product you purchased.
- Your product rating on a scale of 1-5, with 5 being the highest rating.
- Your feedback. It can be long, short, or anything in between. We just want to know your impressions and experience so far with our product. (Good feedback might include how our study material met your needs and ways we might be able to make it even better. You could highlight features that you found helpful or features that you think we should add.)

If you have any questions or concerns, please don't hesitate to contact me directly.

Thanks again!

Sincerely,

Jay Willis
Vice President
<u>jay.willis@mometrix.com</u>
1-800-673-8175

SCAN HERE

M⊘metrix
TEST PREPARATION

The World's #1 Test Preparation Company

Civil Service
Exam Study Guide

Test Prep Secrets for Police Officer, Firefighter, Postal, and More

Over 400 Practice Questions

Step-by-Step Review
Video Tutorials

3rd Edition

Written and edited by the Mometrix Civil Service Test Team

Printed in the United States of America

This paper meets the requirements of ANSI/NISO Z39.48-1992 (Permanence of Paper).

Mometrix offers volume discount pricing to institutions. For more information or a price quote, please contact our sales department at sales@mometrix.com or 888-248-1219.

Mometrix Media LLC is not affiliated with or endorsed by any official testing organization. All organizational and test names are trademarks of their respective owners.

Paperback
ISBN 13: 978-1-5167-1805-4
ISBN 10: 1-5167-1805-4

DEAR FUTURE EXAM SUCCESS STORY

First of all, **THANK YOU** for purchasing Mometrix study materials!

Second, congratulations! You are one of the few determined test-takers who are committed to doing whatever it takes to excel on your exam. **You have come to the right place.** We developed these study materials with one goal in mind: to deliver you the information you need in a format that's concise and easy to use.

In addition to optimizing your guide for the content of the test, we've outlined our recommended steps for breaking down the preparation process into small, attainable goals so you can make sure you stay on track.

We've also analyzed the entire test-taking process, identifying the most common pitfalls and showing how you can overcome them and be ready for any curveball the test throws you.

Standardized testing is one of the biggest obstacles on your road to success, which only increases the importance of doing well in the high-pressure, high-stakes environment of test day. Your results on this test could have a significant impact on your future, and this guide provides the information and practical advice to help you achieve your full potential on test day.

Your success is our success

We would love to hear from you! If you would like to share the story of your exam success or if you have any questions or comments in regard to our products, please contact us at **800-673-8175** or **support@mometrix.com**.

Thanks again for your business and we wish you continued success!

Sincerely,
The Mometrix Test Preparation Team

TABLE OF CONTENTS

Introduction

Thank you for purchasing this resource! You have made the choice to prepare yourself for a test that could have a huge impact on your future, and this guide is designed to help you be fully ready for test day. Obviously, it's important to have a solid understanding of the test material, but you also need to be prepared for the unique environment and stressors of the test, so that you can perform to the best of your abilities.

For this purpose, the first section that appears in this guide is the **Secret Keys**. We've devoted countless hours to meticulously researching what works and what doesn't, and we've boiled down our findings to the five most impactful steps you can take to improve your performance on the test. We start at the beginning with study planning and move through the preparation process, all the way to the testing strategies that will help you get the most out of what you know when you're finally sitting in front of the test.

We recommend that you start preparing for your test as far in advance as possible. However, if you've bought this guide as a last-minute study resource and only have a few days before your test, we recommend that you skip over the first two Secret Keys since they address a long-term study plan.

If you struggle with **test anxiety**, we strongly encourage you to check out our recommendations for how you can overcome it. Test anxiety is a formidable foe, but it can be beaten, and we want to make sure you have the tools you need to defeat it.

Secret Key #1 – Plan Big, Study Small

There's a lot riding on your performance. If you want to ace this test, you're going to need to keep your skills sharp and the material fresh in your mind. You need a plan that lets you review everything you need to know while still fitting in your schedule. We'll break this strategy down into three categories.

Information Organization

Start with the information you already have: the official test outline. From this, you can make a complete list of all the concepts you need to cover before the test. Organize these concepts into groups that can be studied together, and create a list of any related vocabulary you need to learn so you can brush up on any difficult terms. You'll want to keep this vocabulary list handy once you actually start studying since you may need to add to it along the way.

Time Management

Once you have your set of study concepts, decide how to spread them out over the time you have left before the test. Break your study plan into small, clear goals so you have a manageable task for each day and know exactly what you're doing. Then just focus on one small step at a time. When you manage your time this way, you don't need to spend hours at a time studying. Studying a small block of content for a short period each day helps you retain information better and avoid stressing over how much you have left to do. You can relax knowing that you have a plan to cover everything in time. In order for this strategy to be effective though, you have to start studying early and stick to your schedule. Avoid the exhaustion and futility that comes from last-minute cramming!

Study Environment

The environment you study in has a big impact on your learning. Studying in a coffee shop, while probably more enjoyable, is not likely to be as fruitful as studying in a quiet room. It's important to keep distractions to a minimum. You're only planning to study for a short block of time, so make the most of it. Don't pause to check your phone or get up to find a snack. It's also important to **avoid multitasking**. Research has consistently shown that multitasking will make your studying dramatically less effective. Your study area should also be comfortable and well-lit so you don't have the distraction of straining your eyes or sitting on an uncomfortable chair.

 The time of day you study is also important. You want to be rested and alert. Don't wait until just before bedtime. Study when you'll be most likely to comprehend and remember. Even better, if you know what time of day your test will be, set that time aside for study. That way your brain will be used to working on that subject at that specific time and you'll have a better chance of recalling information.

Finally, it can be helpful to team up with others who are studying for the same test. Your actual studying should be done in as isolated an environment as possible, but the work of organizing the information and setting up the study plan can be divided up. In between study sessions, you can discuss with your teammates the concepts that you're all studying and quiz each other on the details. Just be sure that your teammates are as serious about the test as you are. If you find that your study time is being replaced with social time, you might need to find a new team.

Secret Key #2 – Make Your Studying Count

You're devoting a lot of time and effort to preparing for this test, so you want to be absolutely certain it will pay off. This means doing more than just reading the content and hoping you can remember it on test day. It's important to make every minute of study count. There are two main areas you can focus on to make your studying count.

Retention

It doesn't matter how much time you study if you can't remember the material. You need to make sure you are retaining the concepts. To check your retention of the information you're learning, try recalling it at later times with minimal prompting. Try carrying around flashcards and glance at one or two from time to time or ask a friend who's also studying for the test to quiz you.

To enhance your retention, look for ways to put the information into practice so that you can apply it rather than simply recalling it. If you're using the information in practical ways, it will be much easier to remember. Similarly, it helps to solidify a concept in your mind if you're not only reading it to yourself but also explaining it to someone else. Ask a friend to let you teach them about a concept you're a little shaky on (or speak aloud to an imaginary audience if necessary). As you try to summarize, define, give examples, and answer your friend's questions, you'll understand the concepts better and they will stay with you longer. Finally, step back for a big picture view and ask yourself how each piece of information fits with the whole subject. When you link the different concepts together and see them working together as a whole, it's easier to remember the individual components.

Finally, practice showing your work on any multi-step problems, even if you're just studying. Writing out each step you take to solve a problem will help solidify the process in your mind, and you'll be more likely to remember it during the test.

Modality

Modality simply refers to the means or method by which you study. Choosing a study modality that fits your own individual learning style is crucial. No two people learn best in exactly the same way, so it's important to know your strengths and use them to your advantage.

For example, if you learn best by visualization, focus on visualizing a concept in your mind and draw an image or a diagram. Try color-coding your notes, illustrating them, or creating symbols that will trigger your mind to recall a learned concept. If you learn best by hearing or discussing information, find a study partner who learns the same way or read aloud to yourself. Think about how to put the information in your own words. Imagine that you are giving a lecture on the topic and record yourself so you can listen to it later.

For any learning style, flashcards can be helpful. Organize the information so you can take advantage of spare moments to review. Underline key words or phrases. Use different colors for different categories. Mnemonic devices (such as creating a short list in which every item starts with the same letter) can also help with retention. Find what works best for you and use it to store the information in your mind most effectively and easily.

Secret Key #3 – Practice the Right Way

Your success on test day depends not only on how many hours you put into preparing, but also on whether you prepared the right way. It's good to check along the way to see if your studying is paying off. One of the most effective ways to do this is by taking practice tests to evaluate your progress. Practice tests are useful because they show exactly where you need to improve. Every time you take a practice test, pay special attention to these three groups of questions:

- The questions you got wrong
- The questions you had to guess on, even if you guessed right
- The questions you found difficult or slow to work through

This will show you exactly what your weak areas are, and where you need to devote more study time. Ask yourself why each of these questions gave you trouble. Was it because you didn't understand the material? Was it because you didn't remember the vocabulary? Do you need more repetitions on this type of question to build speed and confidence? Dig into those questions and figure out how you can strengthen your weak areas as you go back to review the material.

 Additionally, many practice tests have a section explaining the answer choices. It can be tempting to read the explanation and think that you now have a good understanding of the concept. However, an explanation likely only covers part of the question's broader context. Even if the explanation makes perfect sense, **go back and investigate** every concept related to the question until you're positive you have a thorough understanding.

As you go along, keep in mind that the practice test is just that: practice. Memorizing these questions and answers will not be very helpful on the actual test because it is unlikely to have any of the same exact questions. If you only know the right answers to the sample questions, you won't be prepared for the real thing. **Study the concepts** until you understand them fully, and then you'll be able to answer any question that shows up on the test.

It's important to wait on the practice tests until you're ready. If you take a test on your first day of study, you may be overwhelmed by the amount of material covered and how much you need to learn. Work up to it gradually.

On test day, you'll need to be prepared for answering questions, managing your time, and using the test-taking strategies you've learned. It's a lot to balance, like a mental marathon that will have a big impact on your future. Like training for a marathon, you'll need to start slowly and work your way up. When test day arrives, you'll be ready.

Start with the strategies you've read in the first two Secret Keys—plan your course and study in the way that works best for you. If you have time, consider using multiple study resources to get different approaches to the same concepts. It can be helpful to see difficult concepts from more than one angle. Then find a good source for practice tests. Many times, the test website will suggest potential study resources or provide sample tests.

4

Practice Test Strategy

If you're able to find at least three practice tests, we recommend this strategy:

UNTIMED AND OPEN-BOOK PRACTICE

Take the first test with no time constraints and with your notes and study guide handy. Take your time and focus on applying the strategies you've learned.

TIMED AND OPEN-BOOK PRACTICE

Take the second practice test open-book as well, but set a timer and practice pacing yourself to finish in time.

TIMED AND CLOSED-BOOK PRACTICE

Take any other practice tests as if it were test day. Set a timer and put away your study materials. Sit at a table or desk in a quiet room, imagine yourself at the testing center, and answer questions as quickly and accurately as possible.

Keep repeating timed and closed-book tests on a regular basis until you run out of practice tests or it's time for the actual test. Your mind will be ready for the schedule and stress of test day, and you'll be able to focus on recalling the material you've learned.

Secret Key #4 – Pace Yourself

Once you're fully prepared for the material on the test, your biggest challenge on test day will be managing your time. Just knowing that the clock is ticking can make you panic even if you have plenty of time left. Work on pacing yourself so you can build confidence against the time constraints of the exam. Pacing is a difficult skill to master, especially in a high-pressure environment, so **practice is vital**.

Set time expectations for your pace based on how much time is available. For example, if a section has 60 questions and the time limit is 30 minutes, you know you have to average 30 seconds or less per question in order to answer them all. Although 30 seconds is the hard limit, set 25 seconds per question as your goal, so you reserve extra time to spend on harder questions. When you budget extra time for the harder questions, you no longer have any reason to stress when those questions take longer to answer.

Don't let this time expectation distract you from working through the test at a calm, steady pace, but keep it in mind so you don't spend too much time on any one question. Recognize that taking extra time on one question you don't understand may keep you from answering two that you do understand later in the test. If your time limit for a question is up and you're still not sure of the answer, mark it and move on, and come back to it later if the time and the test format allow. If the testing format doesn't allow you to return to earlier questions, just make an educated guess; then put it out of your mind and move on.

On the easier questions, be careful not to rush. It may seem wise to hurry through them so you have more time for the challenging ones, but it's not worth missing one if you know the concept and just didn't take the time to read the question fully. Work efficiently but make sure you understand the question and have looked at all of the answer choices, since more than one may seem right at first.

Even if you're paying attention to the time, you may find yourself a little behind at some point. You should speed up to get back on track, but do so wisely. Don't panic; just take a few seconds less on each question until you're caught up. Don't guess without thinking, but do look through the answer choices and eliminate any you know are wrong. If you can get down to two choices, it is often worthwhile to guess from those. Once you've chosen an answer, move on and don't dwell on any that you skipped or had to hurry through. If a question was taking too long, chances are it was one of the harder ones, so you weren't as likely to get it right anyway.

On the other hand, if you find yourself getting ahead of schedule, it may be beneficial to slow down a little. The more quickly you work, the more likely you are to make a careless mistake that will affect your score. You've budgeted time for each question, so don't be afraid to spend that time. Practice an efficient but careful pace to get the most out of the time you have.

Secret Key #5 – Have a Plan for Guessing

When you're taking the test, you may find yourself stuck on a question. Some of the answer choices seem better than others, but you don't see the one answer choice that is obviously correct. What do you do?

The scenario described above is very common, yet most test takers have not effectively prepared for it. Developing and practicing a plan for guessing may be one of the single most effective uses of your time as you get ready for the exam.

In developing your plan for guessing, there are three questions to address:

- When should you start the guessing process?
- How should you narrow down the choices?
- Which answer should you choose?

When to Start the Guessing Process

Unless your plan for guessing is to select C every time (which, despite its merits, is not what we recommend), you need to leave yourself enough time to apply your answer elimination strategies. Since you have a limited amount of time for each question, that means that if you're going to give yourself the best shot at guessing correctly, you have to decide quickly whether or not you will guess.

Of course, the best-case scenario is that you don't have to guess at all, so first, see if you can answer the question based on your knowledge of the subject and basic reasoning skills. Focus on the key words in the question and try to jog your memory of related topics. Give yourself a chance to bring the knowledge to mind, but once you realize that you don't have (or you can't access) the knowledge you need to answer the question, it's time to start the guessing process.

It's almost always better to start the guessing process too early than too late. It only takes a few seconds to remember something and answer the question from knowledge. Carefully eliminating wrong answer choices takes longer. Plus, going through the process of eliminating answer choices can actually help jog your memory.

Summary: Start the guessing process as soon as you decide that you can't answer the question based on your knowledge.

7

How to Narrow Down the Choices

The next chapter in this book (**Test-Taking Strategies**) includes a wide range of strategies for how to approach questions and how to look for answer choices to eliminate. You will definitely want to read those carefully, practice them, and figure out which ones work best for you. Here though, we're going to address a mindset rather than a particular strategy.

Your odds of guessing an answer correctly depend on how many options you are choosing from.

Number of options left	5	4	3	2	1
Odds of guessing correctly	20%	25%	33%	50%	100%

You can see from this chart just how valuable it is to be able to eliminate incorrect answers and make an educated guess, but there are two things that many test takers do that cause them to miss out on the benefits of guessing:

- Accidentally eliminating the correct answer
- Selecting an answer based on an impression

We'll look at the first one here, and the second one in the next section.

To avoid accidentally eliminating the correct answer, we recommend a thought exercise called **the $5 challenge**. In this challenge, you only eliminate an answer choice from contention if you are willing to bet $5 on it being wrong. Why $5? Five dollars is a small but not insignificant amount of money. It's an amount you could afford to lose but wouldn't want to throw away. And while losing

$5 once might not hurt too much, doing it twenty times will set you back $100. In the same way, each small decision you make—eliminating a choice here, guessing on a question there—won't by itself impact your score very much, but when you put them all together, they can make a big difference. By holding each answer choice elimination decision to a higher standard, you can reduce the risk of accidentally eliminating the correct answer.

The $5 challenge can also be applied in a positive sense: If you are willing to bet $5 that an answer choice *is* correct, go ahead and mark it as correct.

Summary: Only eliminate an answer choice if you are willing to bet $5 that it is wrong.

8

Which Answer to Choose

You're taking the test. You've run into a hard question and decided you'll have to guess. You've eliminated all the answer choices you're willing to bet $5 on. Now you have to pick an answer. Why do we even need to talk about this? Why can't you just pick whichever one you feel like when the time comes?

The answer to these questions is that if you don't come into the test with a plan, you'll rely on your impression to select an answer choice, and if you do that, you risk falling into a trap. The test writers know that everyone who takes their test will be guessing on some of the questions, so they intentionally write wrong answer choices to seem plausible. You still have to pick an answer though, and if the wrong answer choices are designed to look right, how can you ever be sure that you're not falling for their trap? The best solution we've found to this dilemma is to take the decision out of your hands entirely. Here is the process we recommend:

Once you've eliminated any choices that you are confident (willing to bet $5) are wrong, select the first remaining choice as your answer.

Whether you choose to select the first remaining choice, the second, or the last, the important thing is that you use some preselected standard. Using this approach guarantees that you will not be enticed into selecting an answer choice that looks right, because you are not basing your decision on how the answer choices look.

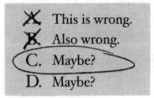

This is not meant to make you question your knowledge. Instead, it is to help you recognize the difference between your knowledge and your impressions. There's a huge difference between thinking an answer is right because of what you know, and thinking an answer is right because it looks or sounds like it should be right.

Summary: To ensure that your selection is appropriately random, make a predetermined selection from among all answer choices you have not eliminated.

Test-Taking Strategies

This section contains a list of test-taking strategies that you may find helpful as you work through the test. By taking what you know and applying logical thought, you can maximize your chances of answering any question correctly!

It is very important to realize that every question is different and every person is different: no single strategy will work on every question, and no single strategy will work for every person. That's why we've included all of them here, so you can try them out and determine which ones work best for different types of questions and which ones work best for you.

Question Strategies

ⓥ READ CAREFULLY

Read the question and the answer choices carefully. Don't miss the question because you misread the terms. You have plenty of time to read each question thoroughly and make sure you understand what is being asked. Yet a happy medium must be attained, so don't waste too much time. You must read carefully and efficiently.

ⓥ CONTEXTUAL CLUES

Look for contextual clues. If the question includes a word you are not familiar with, look at the immediate context for some indication of what the word might mean. Contextual clues can often give you all the information you need to decipher the meaning of an unfamiliar word. Even if you can't determine the meaning, you may be able to narrow down the possibilities enough to make a solid guess at the answer to the question.

ⓥ PREFIXES

If you're having trouble with a word in the question or answer choices, try dissecting it. Take advantage of every clue that the word might include. Prefixes and suffixes can be a huge help. Usually, they allow you to determine a basic meaning. *Pre-* means before, *post-* means after, *pro-* is positive, *de-* is negative. From prefixes and suffixes, you can get an idea of the general meaning of the word and try to put it into context.

ⓥ HEDGE WORDS

Watch out for critical hedge words, such as *likely, may, can, sometimes, often, almost, mostly, usually, generally, rarely,* and *sometimes.* Question writers insert these hedge phrases to cover every possibility. Often an answer choice will be wrong simply because it leaves no room for exception. Be on guard for answer choices that have definitive words such as *exactly* and *always.*

ⓥ SWITCHBACK WORDS

Stay alert for *switchbacks.* These are the words and phrases frequently used to alert you to shifts in thought. The most common switchback words are *but, although,* and *however.* Others include *nevertheless, on the other hand, even though, while, in spite of, despite,* and *regardless of.* Switchback words are important to catch because they can change the direction of the question or an answer choice.

10

☑ Face Value

When in doubt, use common sense. Accept the situation in the problem at face value. Don't read too much into it. These problems will not require you to make wild assumptions. If you have to go beyond creativity and warp time or space in order to have an answer choice fit the question, then you should move on and consider the other answer choices. These are normal problems rooted in reality. The applicable relationship or explanation may not be readily apparent, but it is there for you to figure out. Use your common sense to interpret anything that isn't clear.

Answer Choice Strategies

☑ Answer Selection

The most thorough way to pick an answer choice is to identify and eliminate wrong answers until only one is left, then confirm it is the correct answer. Sometimes an answer choice may immediately seem right, but be careful. The test writers will usually put more than one reasonable answer choice on each question, so take a second to read all of them and make sure that the other choices are not equally obvious. As long as you have time left, it is better to read every answer choice than to pick the first one that looks right without checking the others.

☑ Answer Choice Families

An answer choice family consists of two (in rare cases, three) answer choices that are very similar in construction and cannot all be true at the same time. If you see two answer choices that are direct opposites or parallels, one of them is usually the correct answer. For instance, if one answer choice says that quantity x increases and another either says that quantity x decreases (opposite) or says that quantity y increases (parallel), then those answer choices would fall into the same family. An answer choice that doesn't match the construction of the answer choice family is more likely to be incorrect. Most questions will not have answer choice families, but when they do appear, you should be prepared to recognize them.

☑ Eliminate Answers

Eliminate answer choices as soon as you realize they are wrong, but make sure you consider all possibilities. If you are eliminating answer choices and realize that the last one you are left with is also wrong, don't panic. Start over and consider each choice again. There may be something you missed the first time that you will realize on the second pass.

☑ Avoid Fact Traps

Don't be distracted by an answer choice that is factually true but doesn't answer the question. You are looking for the choice that answers the question. Stay focused on what the question is asking for so you don't accidentally pick an answer that is true but incorrect. Always go back to the question and make sure the answer choice you've selected actually answers the question and is not merely a true statement.

☑ Extreme Statements

In general, you should avoid answers that put forth extreme actions as standard practice or proclaim controversial ideas as established fact. An answer choice that states the "process should be used in certain situations, if…" is much more likely to be correct than one that states the "process should be discontinued completely." The first is a calm rational statement and doesn't even make a definitive, uncompromising stance, using a hedge word *if* to provide wiggle room, whereas the second choice is far more extreme.

11

⊘ Benchmark

As you read through the answer choices and you come across one that seems to answer the question well, mentally select that answer choice. This is not your final answer, but it's the one that will help you evaluate the other answer choices. The one that you selected is your benchmark or standard for judging each of the other answer choices. Every other answer choice must be compared to your benchmark. That choice is correct until proven otherwise by another answer choice beating it. If you find a better answer, then that one becomes your new benchmark. Once you've decided that no other choice answers the question as well as your benchmark, you have your final answer.

⊘ Predict the Answer

Before you even start looking at the answer choices, it is often best to try to predict the answer. When you come up with the answer on your own, it is easier to avoid distractions and traps because you will know exactly what to look for. The right answer choice is unlikely to be word-for-word what you came up with, but it should be a close match. Even if you are confident that you have the right answer, you should still take the time to read each option before moving on.

General Strategies

⊘ Tough Questions

If you are stumped on a problem or it appears too hard or too difficult, don't waste time. Move on! Remember though, if you can quickly check for obviously incorrect answer choices, your chances of guessing correctly are greatly improved. Before you completely give up, at least try to knock out a couple of possible answers. Eliminate what you can and then guess at the remaining answer choices before moving on.

⊘ Check Your Work

Since you will probably not know every term listed and the answer to every question, it is important that you get credit for the ones that you do know. Don't miss any questions through careless mistakes. If at all possible, try to take a second to look back over your answer selection and make sure you've selected the correct answer choice and haven't made a costly careless mistake (such as marking an answer choice that you didn't mean to mark). This quick double check should more than pay for itself in caught mistakes for the time it costs.

⊘ Pace Yourself

It's easy to be overwhelmed when you're looking at a page full of questions; your mind is confused and full of random thoughts, and the clock is ticking down faster than you would like. Calm down and maintain the pace that you have set for yourself. Especially as you get down to the last few minutes of the test, don't let the small numbers on the clock make you panic. As long as you are on track by monitoring your pace, you are guaranteed to have time for each question.

⊘ Don't Rush

It is very easy to make errors when you are in a hurry. Maintaining a fast pace in answering questions is pointless if it makes you miss questions that you would have gotten right otherwise. Test writers like to include distracting information and wrong answers that seem right. Taking a little extra time to avoid careless mistakes can make all the difference in your test score. Find a pace that allows you to be confident in the answers that you select.

⏱ Keep Moving

Panicking will not help you pass the test, so do your best to stay calm and keep moving. Taking deep breaths and going through the answer elimination steps you practiced can help to break through a stress barrier and keep your pace.

Final Notes

The combination of a solid foundation of content knowledge and the confidence that comes from practicing your plan for applying that knowledge is the key to maximizing your performance on test day. As your foundation of content knowledge is built up and strengthened, you'll find that the strategies included in this chapter become more and more effective in helping you quickly sift through the distractions and traps of the test to isolate the correct answer.

Now that you're preparing to move forward into the test content chapters of this book, be sure to keep your goal in mind. As you read, think about how you will be able to apply this information on the test. If you've already seen sample questions for the test and you have an idea of the question format and style, try to come up with questions of your own that you can answer based on what you're reading. This will give you valuable practice applying your knowledge in the same ways you can expect to on test day.

Good luck and good studying!

Civil Service Tests

WHAT ARE CIVIL SERVICE TESTS?

The term "civil service test" can be confusing, but essentially the phrase refers to a test one takes in order to qualify for a government job. These positions may be at the city, county, state, or federal level. Civil service jobs encompass a wide variety of occupations, in every field from administration to zoology. However, not every government job is a civil service job. For some government positions, a person must run for office and win an election. For others, a person must be appointed or recommended by someone in office, and in many cases he/she must be approved or confirmed by an official government agency or board before moving into the position.

Most government jobs, though, are filled through a regular hiring process. When a job opening comes up, it is made public, on government bulletin boards and websites and possibly in local newspapers. In most cases, the job listing will provide an idea of the salary or wage the job offers, and it will also list the minimum requirements a person must have to apply. If an exam is required as part of the application process, this information will also be included. These exams are also known as civil service tests.

You should know that not all civil service positions are referred to as civil service jobs. Sometimes these positions are simply known as "municipal jobs," "state jobs," "county employment," etc. No matter the title, all civil service jobs have two things in common—they are government jobs, and taking some sort of exam is part of the application process.

There are two broad categories of civil service exams—competitive and noncompetitive. On noncompetitive tests, everyone who achieves the minimum passing score or higher will be placed into a pool of people eligible to be hired, on an equal ranking. In other words, if you score a 95 on an exam that requires a passing score of 70, and the person next to you scores a 75, you will both be placed on the eligibility list on an equal footing. Your 95 won't give you an advantage over the person with the 75. On competitive exams, the opposite is true—people who score higher are ranked above those with lower scores. Those with the highest scores are first in line for the next step in the hiring process.

WHY DO WE HAVE CIVIL SERVICE TESTS?

Why do people applying for government jobs have to take a test? There are several good reasons for civil service exams. One of the main ones is to prevent "cronyism," or government officials using their power to give jobs to friends, family members, or anyone else they choose. Cronyism is bad because it's unfair; only people who know the right people have a chance to get a government job. It's also corrupt, because it often leads to hiring in exchange for bribes.

Another negative effect of cronyism is that jobs are staffed with people who aren't very qualified for the position (or even qualified at all). To have good government, it is imperative that only qualified people are hired for government jobs. Preventing cronyism is the reason the civil service exam system was originally developed in the United States.

Besides preventing cronyism and making sure that only qualified people are hired, civil service testing provides another valuable function for government agencies. Government jobs are highly sought after; in many cities it's not unusual to have thousands of applicants for a government job. By requiring people to achieve minimum scores on civil service tests, governments save countless man-hours that would otherwise be spent reviewing resumes and interviewing people who turn out to be unqualified.

WHAT ARE CIVIL SERVICE TESTS LIKE?

Like the jobs they test for, civil service exams come in many different forms. Some exams are very job specific, designed and written to test for advanced levels of knowledge and skills in a particular area. Others are much broader, measuring a person's general skills and knowledge in subjects such as language, math, reading comprehension, writing, making decisions, etc. Most civil service exams fall into the latter category, and those are the tests this guide is focused on. Of course, if you're taking a more specialized exam, this guide can also be very helpful, because it's likely that some portion of the test will be on general subjects.

Even on the general knowledge exams, the degree of difficulty can vary widely. Reading comprehension portions, for example, can range from tests that simply measure a person's ability to understand basic, written information to exams that require the test taker to have a highly advanced vocabulary and to be able to make well-reasoned, logical inferences based on the text. Of course, no matter how hard the civil service test is, you can significantly improve your chances of achieving a high score by relying on this guide to help you prepare.

The test format will almost always be multiple-choice. This is because anywhere from dozens to thousands of people will take the same test, so government agencies need an exam that doesn't require each test form to be reviewed and scored by hand. Multiple-choice tests are easily scored, making the task easier, faster, and less expensive.

On the majority of civil service exams, there is only one answer for each question, but that's not always true, so you need to read the instructions carefully. On occasion the instructions will tell you to "select all that apply," which means there might be more than one correct answer.

On most tests, applicants will be told to select "the correct answer," which means that one answer will clearly stand out from the others as being the only correct one. However, some tests will require the test taker to select "the best answer," which does not mean the same thing. On these questions, one or two of the wrong answer choices will be close to being correct, or even partially correct, but they won't be quite as satisfactory as the correct answer. On these kinds of questions, you'll want to spend a bit more time weighing the choices before making your selection.

Another thing to keep in mind is that on most civil service exams, the test taker will have four answer choices to choose from, while a few tests will offer five answer choices. Those with five choices aren't necessarily harder than those with only four, so if you encounter one of the exams with five answer choices, there's no need to worry. Even on tests with only four answer choices, it's difficult for test designers to come up with four different answers that sound right. Usually at least one answer is clearly wrong to anyone who has any familiarity with the subject. On tests with five choices, there will usually be two answers that are obviously wrong. This won't always be the case, but most of the time, no matter how many answer choices each question has, there will only be two or three that are actually plausible.

Many civil service exams are taken the old-fashioned way, with pencil and paper, but a growing number are now taken on a computer. You don't need any special computer skills to take a general civil service test electronically, as you'll be given all the instructions you need at the test center. Of course, if the job you're applying for requires advanced computer skills, this may not be true. Be sure to read the test details carefully before applying to take any civil service exam.

There are two kinds of computer-based exams. Most are simply electronic versions of the pencil and paper version, with no other differences. There's another kind, though, called computer adaptive tests, and there are major differences between these and the pencil and paper tests. On these exams, the first question you see is one of medium difficulty; test designers will make sure it's neither very easy nor very hard.

The next question you see will depend on your answer to the first question. If you answer incorrectly, you'll get an easier question. If you answer correctly, you'll get a harder question. (However, you won't know if you answered a question correctly or not.) This process continues for the entire test—correct answers lead to harder questions, while incorrect answers lead to easier questions. In other words, the computer adapts the test to your responses. Naturally, the harder questions count more when it comes to scoring the test.

How Do I Take a Civil Service Test?

How you'll go about taking a civil service exam depends on many factors. There are thousands of different civil service tests given every year in America at the federal, state, and local levels. They are given throughout the year and in hundreds of locations. Some are given only when the pool of people who are eligible to be hired drops below a certain point. Others are given on a regular basis, usually once or twice a year. You'll need to go online and look up the exact information for the positions you're interested in.

Civil Service Job Sites

Almost all civil service job openings are listed online now, usually on a page of the official site of the government entity. We haven't listed the official civil service webpage for every city and county government in the US in this guide, because this would take hundreds of pages. You can find the online list of civil service jobs, salaries, requirements, test dates, etc., in your area by simply going to a search engine and entering the phrase "government jobs" along with the name of the county or city you're interested in working for. If you don't have access to a computer, simply call or visit the county courthouse or municipal building to find out where you can view the information in person.

Keep in mind that there are federal jobs all over the country, not just in Washington, D.C. Also, if you live close to the border of another state, and you're willing to drive (or move) for the right job offer, you should consider taking civil service tests in that state, too. A few states require civil service employees to actually live in the state, but most do not. Also, some states break down job listings by region. In this case, make sure you're applying for jobs only in regions where you want to work.

Finally, if you're planning on applying for more than one job, in the same state or in different states, don't forget that civil service exams are not all alike. They can vary widely, job by job or state by state. Don't assume that if you're applying for a secretarial position in two states that the civil service exams will be identical. They might be quite similar, but they might be quite different, too. The same holds true if you're applying for two different maintenance positions in the same state— the tests could be exactly the same, but that's not necessarily the case. Always check the official job listings for more information about the required test.

Here are the websites for civil service jobs for all 50 states, the District of Columbia, and the federal government.

Federal Jobs   https://www.usajobs.gov/

Alabama   https://joblink.alabama.gov/ada/

Alaska	http://jobs.alaska.gov/statejobs.html
Arizona	http://www.hr.az.gov/AZStateJobs/
Arkansas	https://www.ark.org/arstatejobs/index.php
California	http://jobs.ca.gov/
Colorado	http://agency.governmentjobs.com/colorado/default.cfm
Connecticut	http://das.ct.gov/cr1.aspx?page=13
Delaware	http://delawarestatejobs.com/
District of Columbia	http://dchr.dc.gov/page/careers
Florida	https://peoplefirst.myflorida.com/peoplefirst
Georgia	http://team.georgia.gov/careers/
Hawaii	http://agency.governmentjobs.com/hawaii/default.cfm
Idaho	https://dhr.idaho.gov/JobSeekers/StateJobOpenings.html
Illinois	http://work.illinois.gov/
Indiana	http://www.in.gov/spd/2334.htm
Iowa	https://das.iowa.gov/human-resources/state-employment
Kansas	http://da.ks.gov/ps/aaa/recruitment/
Kentucky	https://careers.ky.gov/Pages/default.aspx
Louisiana	http://www.civilservice.louisiana.gov/
Maine	http://www.maine.gov/bhr/state_jobs/index.htm
Maryland	http://www.dbm.maryland.gov/jobseekers/Pages/JobSearch.aspx
Massachusetts	https://massanf.taleo.net/careersection/ex/joblist.ftl
Michigan	http://agency.governmentjobs.com/michigan/default.cfm
Minnesota	https://mn.gov/mmb/careers/search-for-jobs/
Mississippi	http://www.mspb.ms.gov/
Missouri	https://www.mo.gov/work/job-seekers/state-job-openings/
Montana	http://mt.gov/statejobs/default.mcpx
Nebraska	http://statejobs.nebraska.gov/
Nevada	http://nv.gov/employment/

New Hampshire	https://das.nh.gov/
New Jersey	http://www.state.nj.us/nj/employ/
New Mexico	http://www.spo.state.nm.us/
New York	http://www.labor.ny.gov/jobs/regional.shtm
North Carolina	http://www.osp.state.nc.us/jobs/
North Dakota	http://www.nd.gov/category.htm?id=95
Ohio	https://www.governmentjobs.com/careers/ohio
Oklahoma	http://www.ok.gov/opm/State_Jobs/
Oregon	http://www.oregon.gov/DAS/STJOBS/Pages/index.aspx
Pennsylvania	http://www.employment.pa.gov/Pages/jobopportunities.aspx
Rhode Island	http://www.dlt.ri.gov/jobsri/
South Carolina	http://www.jobs.sc.gov/OHR/OHR-jobs-portal-index.phtm
South Dakota	http://sd.gov/employment.aspx
Tennessee	https://www.tn.gov/hr/section/employment
Texas	http://www.twc.state.tx.us/jobseekers/job-search
Utah	https://agency.governmentjobs.com/utah/default.cfm
Vermont	http://humanresources.vermont.gov/
Virginia	http://jobs.virginia.gov/
Washington	http://www.careers.wa.gov/
West Virginia	http://www.personnel.wv.gov/job_seekers/Pages/default.aspx
Wisconsin	http://wisc.jobs/public/index.asp
Wyoming	http://wyoming.gov/

Word Relationship Questions—Spelling and Vocabulary

In all civil service jobs, communication abilities are extremely important, whether the position is considered skilled or unskilled. If you're hired for a government job, there's a good chance that you'll be interacting with the public as part of the job. You'll also be required to communicate with colleagues and superiors frequently. Good communication skills will enable you to perform your job smoothly and efficiently, get along well with your coworkers and bosses, and create a positive impression on members of the public.

Whether spoken or written, words are at the heart of all communication, so having good verbal skills is essential. You'll need to be able to express yourself clearly as well as to easily grasp what a coworker or manager is trying to say. This is why questions that test your skill with words constitute such a big part of the civil service exam. They're on the test to weed out people who don't have the verbal skills necessary for success on the job.

You'll be tested on your spelling abilities. Why is good spelling important in this day and age when nearly all written communication is done on computers, and nearly all of them have spell checkers? Spelling skills are important because they demonstrate that you have good, basic intelligence and that you have done a fair amount of reading. Knowing how to spell correctly is one of the marks of a person with a well-rounded education. While it's true that there are some very smart people who are not very good spellers, these are the exception, not the rule. Generally speaking, smart people are good spellers, and vice versa.

Spell checkers are certainly very useful tools, but they weren't designed to eliminate the need for good spelling. Their purpose is to call the typist's attention to the occasional mistake that might be easily overlooked, not to replace the typist. Every time the spell checker flags a word, the typist has to click either *Replace* or *Ignore*, and that takes time. With one or two errors, it doesn't take very long, of course, but a person with poor spelling skills would use up a significant amount of time correcting mistakes, even with a spell checker. This would have a negative impact on productivity. Additionally, a spell checker won't catch a word that is spelled correctly but is the wrong one (such as to/too/two). Good spelling skills are very important in civil service jobs, and you should expect to see a lot of spelling questions on the exam.

You'll also be tested for vocabulary, which measures your knowledge of word meanings. Your vocabulary is simply the total of the words you recognize and understand. Keep in mind that if a word is in your vocabulary it doesn't necessarily mean that you hear, read, write, or speak that word on a regular basis. (The words you use on a regular basis are known as your working vocabulary.)

There are thousands of words we don't encounter regularly, but we still need to know the meaning of many of these. Many of the words you'll see on the vocabulary section of your civil service test will fall into this category —words most people don't use in everyday conversation with their families and friends, but that might come up from time to time on the job or while reading. It will be fairly easy to understand how knowing the meaning of these words is important for a civil service position. However, it is certain that you'll also run into some words on the exam that you are very unlikely to encounter on the job.

So, if these words aren't going to come up in the course of your job duties, why are they on the civil service exam? They're on the test because they serve a very useful function for government agencies that use these exams as part of the hiring process. A person's vocabulary is a very good measuring stick of his/her overall knowledge and intelligence. With very few exceptions, an extensive vocabulary is a mark of someone who is very intelligent. This is only logical—the more words a person knows, the more reading he/she has done, and the more subjects and fields he/she is familiar with. Generally speaking, employers would prefer to hire people with above-average levels of knowledge and intelligence, and that's why you'll see unusual and rarely used vocabulary words on the exam.

Also, a person with a large vocabulary will generally be a more effective communicator. A person with a limited vocabulary will have a hard time understanding others and clearly expressing himself precisely because he doesn't know the meaning of a lot of words. There's no need to panic, though. You won't be required to possess the vocabulary of a Harvard professor in order to do well on the civil service exam. You will just need a vocabulary that's pretty good. If you don't think yours measures up, the practice questions in this guide can help remedy that.

Some of the vocabulary questions you'll see will simply show you a word, and then ask you to select the answer choice that is the correct meaning of the word. Here's an example:

1. Crevice is closest in meaning to:
   a. a serving platter
   b. a large hole
   c. a narrow opening
   d. the fringe on a drape

The basic vocabulary questions on the test you take might have a slightly different format. There may be three answer choices, or possibly five. Instead of standing alone, the word may be used in a sentence. The answer choices might have slightly longer definitions. However, there won't be any major differences, as this is the standard setup for a straightforward vocabulary question.

Spelling Primer

SPELLING RULES
WORDS ENDING WITH A CONSONANT
Usually the final consonant is doubled on a word before adding a suffix. This is the rule for single syllable words, words ending with one consonant, and multi-syllable words with the last syllable accented. For example:

- *beg* becomes *begging* (single syllable)
- *shop* becomes *shopped* (single syllable)
- *add* becomes *adding* (already ends in double consonant, do not add another "d")
- *deter* becomes *deterring* (multi-syllable, accent on last syllable)
- *regret* becomes *regrettable* (multi-syllable, accent on last syllable)
- *compost* becomes *composting* (do not add another "t" because the accent is on the first syllable)

Words Ending in Y and C

The general rule for words ending in *y* is to keep the *y* when adding a suffix if the *y* is preceded by a vowel. If the word ends in a consonant and *y*, the *y* is changed to an *i* before the suffix is added (unless the suffix itself begins with *i*). The following are examples:

- *pay* becomes *paying* (keep the *y*)
- *bully* becomes *bullied* (change to *i*)
- *bully* becomes *bullying* (keep the *y* because the suffix begins with *i*)

If a word ends with *c* and the suffix begins with an *e*, *i*, or *y*, the letter *k* is usually added to the end of the word. The following are examples:

- panic becomes panicky
- mimic becomes mimicking

Words Ending in IE, EI, and E

Most words are spelled with an *i* before *e*, except when they follow the letter *c* OR sound like a long *a*. For example, the following words are spelled correctly according to these rules:

- piece, friend, believe (i before e)
- receive, ceiling, conceited (except after c)
- weight, neighborhood, veil (sounds like a)

To add a suffix to words ending with the letter *e*, first determine if the *e* is silent. If it is, the *e* will be kept if the added suffix begins with a consonant. If the suffix begins with a vowel, the *e* is dropped. For example:

- *age* becomes *ageless* (keep the *e*)
- *age* becomes *aging* (drop the *e*)

An exception to this rule occurs when the word ends in *ce* or *ge* and the suffix *able* or *ous* is added; these words will retain the letter *e*. The following are examples:

- courage becomes courageous
- notice becomes noticeable

Words Ending with ISE and IZE

A small number of words end with *ise*. A much more common ending in American English is *ize*. The following are examples of the first group:

- advertise, advise, arise, chastise, circumcise, and comprise
- compromise, demise, despise, devise, disguise, enterprise, excise, and exercise
- franchise, improvise, incise, merchandise, premise, reprise, and revise
- supervise, surmise, surprise, and televise

Words that end with *ize* include the following:

- accessorize, agonize, authorize, and brutalize
- capitalize, caramelize, categorize, civilize, and demonize
- downsize, empathize, euthanize, idolize, and immunize

- legalize, metabolize, mobilize, organize, and ostracize
- plagiarize, privatize, utilize, and visualize

(Note that some words may technically be spelled with *ise*, especially in British English, but it is more common to use *ize*. Examples include *symbolize/symbolise,* and *baptize/baptise*.)

Words Ending with CEED, SEDE, AND CEDE

Only three words end with *ceed* in the English language: *exceed, proceed,* and *succeed*. There is only one word that ends with *sede*, and that word is *supersede*. Many words end with *cede*, such as *concede, recede,* and *precede*.

Words Ending in ABLE OR IBLE

For words ending in *able* or *ible*, there are no hard and fast rules. There are more words ending in *able* than *ible*. This is useful information if guessing becomes necessary. The following are examples:

- adjustable, unbeatable, collectable, deliverable, and likeable
- edible, compatible, feasible, sensible, and credible

Words Ending in ANCE AND ENCE

The suffixes *ence, ency,* and *ent* are used in the following cases:

- the suffix is preceded by the letter *c* but sounds like *s—innocence*
- the suffix is preceded by the letter *g* but sounds like *j—intelligent, negligence*

The suffixes *ance, ancy,* and *ant* are used in the following cases:

- the suffix is preceded by the letter *c* but sounds like *k—significant, vacancy*
- the suffix is preceded by the letter *g* with a hard sound—*elegant, extravagance*

If the suffix is preceded by other letters, there are no firm rules. For example: *finance* and *defendant* use the letter *a*, while *respondent, competence,* and *excellent* use the letter *e*.

Words Ending in TION, SION, AND CIAN

The word endings *tion, sion,* and *cian* all sound like *shun* or *zhun*. There are no rules for which ending is used for words. The following are examples:

- action, agitation, caution, fiction, nation, and motion
- admission, expression, mansion, permission, and television
- *electrician, magician, musician, optician,* and *physician* (note that these words tend to describe occupations)

Words with the AI OR IA Combination

When deciding if *ai* or *ia* is correct, the combination of *ai* usually sounds like one vowel sound, as in *Britain*, while the vowels in *ia* are pronounced separately, as in *guardian*. The following are examples:

- captain, certain, faint, hair, malaise, and praise (ai makes one sound)
- beneficiary, certifiable, civilian, humiliation, and abbreviate (ia makes two sounds)

PLURAL FORMS OF NOUNS
NOUNS ENDING IN CH, SH, S, X, OR Z
When a noun ends in the letters *ch*, *sh*, *s*, *x*, or *z*, an *es* instead of a single *s* is added to the end of the word to make it plural. The following are examples:

- church becomes churches
- bush becomes bushes
- bass becomes basses
- mix becomes mixes
- buzz becomes buzzes

This is the rule with proper names as well; *the Ross family* would become *the Rosses*.

NOUNS ENDING IN Y
If a noun ends with a consonant and *y*, the plural is formed by replacing the *y* with *ies*. For example, *fly* becomes *flies* and *puppy* becomes *puppies*.

If a noun ends with a vowel and *y*, the plural is formed by adding an *s*. For example, *alley* becomes *alleys* and *boy* becomes *boys*.

NOUNS ENDING IN F OR FE
Most nouns ending in *f* or *fe* are pluralized by replacing the *f* with *v* and adding *es*. For example, *knife* becomes *knives*, *self* becomes *selves*, and *wolf* becomes *wolves*.

An exception to this rule is the word *roof*, which becomes *roofs*.

NOUNS ENDING IN O
Most nouns ending with a consonant and *o* are pluralized by adding *es*. For example, *hero* becomes *heroes*, *tornado* becomes *tornadoes*, and *potato* becomes *potatoes*.

Most nouns ending with a vowel and *o* are pluralized by adding *s*. For example, *portfolio* becomes *portfolios*, *radio* becomes *radios*, and *shoe* becomes *shoes*.

An exception to these rules is seen with musical terms ending in *o*. These words are pluralized by adding *s* even if they end in a consonant and *o*. For example, *soprano* becomes *sopranos*, *banjo* becomes *banjos*, and *piano* becomes *pianos*.

EXCEPTIONS TO THE RULES OF PLURALS
Some words do not fall into any specific category for making the singular form plural. They are irregular. Certain words become plural by changing the vowels within the word. For example, *woman* becomes *women*, *goose* becomes *geese*, and *foot* becomes *feet*.

Some words become completely different words in the plural form. For example, *mouse* becomes *mice*, *fungus* becomes *fungi*, and *alumnus* becomes *alumni*.

Some words are the same in both the singular and plural forms. *Salmon*, *species*, and *deer* are the same, singular or plural.

Plural Forms of Letters, Numbers, Symbols, and Compound Nouns with Hyphens

Letters and numbers become plural by adding an apostrophe and *s*. The following are examples:

- The L's are the people whose names begin with the letter L.
- They broke the teams down into groups of 3's.
- The sorority girls were all KD's.

A compound noun is comprised of two or more words that can be written with hyphens. For example, *mother-in-law* and *court-martial* are compound nouns. To make them plural, an *s* or *es* is added to the main word. *Mother-in-law* becomes *mothers-in-law* and *court-martial* becomes *court-martials*.

accidentally	characteristic	dissipate	hoping	ninety
accommodate	chauffeur	drudgery	hurriedly	noticeable
accompanied	colonel	ecstasy	hygiene	notoriety
accompany	column	efficient	hypocrisy	obedience
achieved	commit	eighth	imminent	obstacle
acknowledgment	committee	eligible	incidentally	occasion
across	comparative	embarrass	incredible	occurrence
address	compel	emphasize	independent	omitted
aggravate	competent	especially	indigestible	operate
aisle	competition	exaggerate	inevitable	optimistic
ancient	conceive	exceed	innocence	organization
anxiety	congratulations	exhaust	intelligible	outrageous
apparently	conqueror	exhilaration	intentionally	pageant
appearance	conscious	existence	intercede	pamphlet
arctic	coolly	explanation	interest	parallel
argument	correspondent	extraordinary	irresistible	parliament
arrangement	courtesy	familiar	judgment	permissible
attendance	curiosity	fascinate	legitimate	perseverance
auxiliary	cylinder	February	liable	persuade
awkward	deceive	fiery	library	physically
bachelor	deference	finally	likelihood	physician
barbarian	deferred	forehead	literature	possess
beggar	definite	foreign	maintenance	possibly
beneficiary	describe	foreigner	maneuver	practically
biscuit	desirable	foremost	manual	prairie
brilliant	desperate	forfeit	mathematics	preceding
business	develop	ghost	mattress	prejudice
cafeteria	diphtheria	glamorous	miniature	prevalent
calendar	disappear	government	mischievous	professor
campaign	disappoint	grammar	misspell	pronouncement
candidate	disastrous	grateful	momentous	pronunciation
ceiling	discipline	grief	mortgage	propeller
cemetery	discussion	grievous	neither	protein
changeable	disease	handkerchief	nickel	psychiatrist
changing	dissatisfied	harass	niece	psychology
quantity	restaurant	sheriff	symmetry	usage
questionnaire	rhetoric	shriek	temperament	vacuum
rally	rhythm	similar	temperature	valuable

recede	ridiculous	soliloquy	tendency	vengeance
receive	sacrilegious	sophomore	tournament	vigilance
recognize	salary	species	tragedy	villain
recommend	scarcely	strenuous	transferred	Wednesday
referral	schedule	studying	truly	weird
referred	secretary	suffrage	twelfth	wholly
relieve	sentinel	supersede	tyranny	yolk
religious	separate	suppress	unanimous	
resistance	severely	surprise	unpleasant	

Spelling and Vocabulary Practice Test

Choose the correct spelling of the missing word.

1. John prefers _____ art to the classics.
   a. Contemporary
   b. Contemperary
   c. Contemparary
   d. Conteporary

2. Allen told Steve that he would give him the ____ version of the story when he had time.
   a. Unabridgged
   b. Unabriddged
   c. Unabbridged
   d. Unabridged

3. Lisa was known for having _____ relationships.
   a. Promiscous
   b. Promicuous
   c. Promiscuous
   d. Promicious

4. The new tax was passed for ____ the waterfront district.
   a. Revitallizing
   b. Revitalizzing
   c. Revitelizing
   d. Revitalizing

5. The increased _____ to the class fund allowed for an end-of-year party.
   a. Revenuee
   b. Revenue
   c. Revanue
   d. Revanuee

6. The teenager ____ some candy from the grocery store.
   a. Pillferred
   b. Pilferred
   c. Pillfered
   d. Pilfered

7. As he was from a small town, some of Dean's views were _____.
   a. Parochial
   b. Perochial
   c. Porochial
   d. Parochiel

8. All of the students dreaded the quizzes the professor gave since he tested on ____ material.

a. Obscere
b. Obscore
c. Obbscure
d. Obscure

9. The judge sued the newspaper for ___.

a. Libel
b. Labal
c. Lobel
d. Libbel

10. Susan's ____ of darkness prevents her from leaving her house at night.

a. Abhorance
b. Abhorence
c. Abhorrence
d. Abhorrance

11. The girl was ____ when she found out her puppy was injured.

a. Destraught
b. Distaught
c. Distraught
d. Distrauht

12. The ____ crowd mourned the loss of their leader.

a. Sember
b. Somber
c. Sombar
d. Sombor

13. The ____ Southern girl was known for her polite behavior.

a. Gentell
b. Ganteel
c. Genteal
d. Genteel

14. The mother attempted to ____ her son with toys.

a. Molifey
b. Mollify
c. Molify
d. Mollifey

15. Some people accused John of thinking too much. He would sometimes ___ a subject for months at a time.

a. Pondar
b. Pondder
c. Ponnder
d. Ponder

16. The young artist had an _____ passion for watercolors.

    a. Unbradled
    b. Unbriddled
    c. Unbridled
    d. Unbridlled

17. The _____ kept the students cool while they sat outside studying.

    a. Zephyir
    b. Zepheyer
    c. Zepyr
    d. Zephyr

18. The pianist played his rendition of a _____.

    a. Sonata
    b. Sonatta
    c. Sonate
    d. Sonete

19. The entertainer had no _____ about performing in front of two thousand screaming fans.

    a. Qulams
    b. Quelms
    c. Qualms
    d. Qualmes

20. The _____ still enjoyed being around its mother but was growing more independent each day.

    a. Yearling
    b. Yeerling
    c. Yearlling
    d. Yearlinng

Spelling and Vocabulary Answer Key and Explanations

1. A: *Contemporary* is the correct spelling. It means up-to-date, modern, or new. In the sentence, a contrast is being drawn with "the classics," which are older pieces of art.

2. D: *Unabridged* is the correct spelling. It means unshortened, complete, or full length. As an example, long books are sometimes sold in "abridged" versions, meaning that they are edited and shortened. In the example sentence, Allen says he needs more time to give the story, suggesting that he means the full version.

3. C: *Promiscuous* is the correct spelling. This word is used to describe people who have casual romantic relationships with a number of different people. It has a generally negative connotation.

4. D: *Revitalizing* is the correct spelling. It means life-restoring or enlivening. It is apparent from the context of this sentence that the waterfront district has been moribund (depressed and dying) and that the government is attempting to stimulate the economy through taxation.

5. B: *Revenue* is the correct spelling. It is defined as money earned through economic activity. A general equation for profit is revenue minus expenses. The revenue earned by the class would make it possible for them to have a party at the end of the year.

6. D: *Pilfered* is the correct spelling. It means stolen. The teenager in the sentence is performing some petty shoplifting at the local store.

7. A: *Parochial* is the correct spelling. It means locally focused or innocent of the ways of the world. A parochial person is unsophisticated and perhaps naive. Being parochial is not necessarily negative, though the word is often used in a critical fashion. A person like Dean who grew up and continued to live in a small town might not take an interest in the outside world, and might therefore be considered parochial.

8. D: *Obscure* is the correct spelling. It means hard to find, uncommon, or rare. Many students have experienced the dread of taking tests from a teacher who includes not just the most important information, but also the random bits of knowledge that are easy to forget.

9. A: *Libel* is the correct spelling. A libel is a false or misleading statement that injures the reputation of another person or group. It is illegal to make or publish such statements.

10. C: *Abhorrence* is the correct spelling. It means hatred or distaste. This makes sense, as a hatred of darkness would prevent one from leaving the house at night.

11. C: *Distraught* is the correct spelling. This word means traumatized, violently emotional, or severely sad and angry. The injury of a pet could make a person distraught.

12. B: *Somber* is the correct spelling. This word means sad or mournful. A group whose leader has died would certainly be somber.

13. D: *Genteel* is the correct spelling. It means sophisticated, classy, or well-bred. Southern women are stereotyped as being demure, well-mannered, and classy, so genteel would be a good fit in this sentence.

14. B: *Mollify* is the correct spelling. To mollify someone is to diminish his/her anger and appease him/her. The parents of young children get a great deal of practice in mollifying their sons and daughters after fits and temper tantrums.

15. D: *Ponder* is the correct spelling. It means to think, meditate, or ruminate. In general, it is good to be a person who ponders, though excessive analysis and thinking can sometimes stand in the way of necessary action.

16. C: *Unbridled* is the correct spelling. It means unrestrained or excessive. A bridle is used to restrain a fast horse, so an unbridled horse will run fast and loose. The word's usage has expanded to include many things besides horses.

17. D: *Zephyr* is the correct spelling. This uncommon word means a west wind.

18. A: *Sonata* is the correct spelling. A sonata is a piece of music written for one or two instruments.

19. C: *Qualms* is the correct spelling. Qualms are reservations or doubts. An experienced performer might not feel any anxiety about performing, even before a very large crowd.

20. A: *Yearling* is the correct spelling. A yearling is a young horse or other animal. Although horses grow up faster than infant humans, a year-old horse might still be afraid to go out entirely on its own.

Spelling Only Practice Test

Each question gives three different spellings of a word. Two are incorrect and one is correct. Select the choice from each set of three that is spelled correctly.

1. A. separate   B. seperate   C. sepparate

2. A. nucular   B. nuclear   C. nuculear

3. A. fermiliar   B. farmiliar   C. familiar

4. A. sacrilegious   B. sacreligious   C. sacraligious

5. A. aggitated   B. agittated   C. agitated

6. A. orientated   B. oriented   C. oreinted

7. A. indispensible   B. indespensible   C. indispensable

8. A. similar   B. simular   C. similiar

9. A. atitude   B. attitude   C. atittude

10. A. abreviate   B. abbreviate   C. abreeviate

11. A. absorb   B. apsorb   C. abzorb

12. A. acumulate   B. acummulate   C. accumulate

13. A. airial   B. aireal   C. aerial

14. A. comedian   B. commedian   C. comedien

15. A. ashphalt   B. asphalt   C. aspalt

16. A. forcable   B. forcible   C. forceble

17. A. anicdote   B. antecdote   C. anecdote

18. A. flexible   B. flexable   C. flexiable

19. A. defendant   B. defendent   C. difendent

20. A. plainteff   B. plaintif   C. plaintiff

21. A. idiocincrasy   B. idiosyncrasy   C. idiosincracy

22. A. hazardous   B. hazerdous   C. hazzardous

23. A. horific   B. horrific   C. horriffic

24. A. hansome   B. handsom   C. handsome

25. A. liaison   B. liason   C. leiaison

26. A. galexy   B. galaxy   C. gallaxy

27. A. attorneys   B. atorneys   C. attornys

28. A. asteriks   B. asterix   C. asterisk

29. A. equalibrium   B. equilibrum   C. equilibrium

30. A. brilliance   B. brillance   C. briliance

31. A. blanche   B. blanch   C. blance

32. A. ecstasy   B. extasy   C. ecstacy

33. A. deppreciate   B. depreciate   C. deappreciate

34. A. terpitude   B. turpittude   C. turpitude

35. A. oposite   B. opposite   C. opossite

36. A. tyrrany   B. tyrranny   C. tyranny

37. A. schism   B. scism   C. shism

38. A. scedule   B. shedule   C. schedule

39. A. incandescent   B. incandesent   C. incandecent

40. A. teriffic   B. terrific   C. terriffic

41. A. homogeneize   B. homogenize   C. homoginise

42. A. sieve   B. seive   C. sive

43. A. truely   B. truley   C. truly

44. A. sincerely   B. sincerly   C. sinceerly

45. A. transeint   B. transient   C. transhent

46. A. sedition   B. sidition   C. sadition

47. A. theives   B. thiefs   C. thieves

48. A. vengance   B. vengeance   C. vengence

49. A. nilon   B. nylon   C. nyllon

50. A. unnacceptable   B. unaceptible   C. unacceptable

51. A. deficit   B. defecit   C. defficit

52. A. disaproval   B. disapproval   C. dissaproval

53. A. diffidence   B. difidence   C. diffedince

54. A. picknicking   B. picnicing   C. picnicking

55. A. orregano   B. oreganno   C. oregano

56. A. batchelor   B. bachelor   C. bachler

57. A. indelible   B. indelable   C. indellible

58. A. dyurnal   B. diurnal   C. dayernal

59. A. impatience   B. impatiense   C. empatiance

60. A. parlament   B. parliment   C. parliament

Spelling Only Answer Key

1. A: separate
2. B: nuclear
3. C: familiar
4. A: sacrilegious
5. C: agitated
6. B: oriented
7. C: indispensable
8. A: similar
9. B: attitude
10. B: abbreviate
11. A: absorb
12. C: accumulate
13. C: aerial
14. A: comedian
15. B: asphalt
16. B: forcible
17. C: anecdote
18. A: flexible
19. A: defendant
20. C: plaintiff
21. B: idiosyncrasy
22. A: hazardous
23. B: horrific
24. C: handsome
25. A: liaison

26. B: galaxy
27. A: attorneys
28. C: asterisk
29. C: equilibrium
30. A: brilliance
31. B: blanch.
32. A: ecstasy
33. B: depreciate
34. C: turpitude
35. B: opposite
36. C: tyranny
37. A: schism
38. C: schedule
39. A: incandescent
40. B: terrific
41. B: homogenize
42. A: sieve
43. C: truly
44. A: sincerely
45. B: transient
46. A: sedition
47. C: thieves
48. B: vengeance
49. B: nylon
50. C: unacceptable

51. A: deficit
52. B: disapproval
53. A: diffidence
54. C: picnicking
55. C: oregano
56. B: bachelor
57. A: indelible
58. B: diurnal
59. A: impatience
60. C: parliament

35

Vocabulary Practice Test 1

For each word, choose the answer that contains the word or phrase that is closest in meaning.

1. Elucidate

    a. to complain
    b. to escape
    c. to explain
    d. to extract

2. Accord

    a. plan
    b. agreement
    c. rope
    d. skill

3. Annual

    a. to declare void
    b. around Christmas time
    c. new
    d. yearly

4. Scarce

    a. rare
    b. plentiful
    c. odd
    d. ferocious

5. Convince

    a. to deceive
    b. to persuade
    c. to accuse
    d. to harass

6. Incite

    a. understanding
    b. to provoke
    c. to delay
    d. to remove

7. Invoke

    a. to create
    b. to appeal to
    c. to twist
    d. to reverse

8. Haughty

    a. arrogant
    b. confused
    c. mild
    d. very large

9. Dubious

    a. remarkable
    b. silent
    c. tricky
    d. questionable

10. Novel

    a. unusual
    b. ordinary
    c. popular
    d. boring

11. Bequeath

    a. to quiver
    b. to give
    c. under
    d. to take unlawfully

12. Disdain

    a. contempt
    b. concern
    c. fragility
    d. remorse

13. Compel

    a. to measure against
    b. to rethink
    c. to force
    d. to move fast

14. Illustrious

    a. generous
    b. celebrated
    c. expensive
    d. very ill

15. Mortify

    a. to refrigerate
    b. to apply
    c. to strengthen
    d. to embarrass

16. Authorize
a. to approve
b. to seal by burning
c. to make louder
d. to steal

17. Penchant
a. necklace
b. wealthy
c. accent
d. tendency

18. Capitulate
a. to reduce in size
b. to repeat
c. to agree to
d. to surrender

19. Imbibe
a. to drink
b. to offer money to
c. to include
d. to follow behind

20. Bucolic
a. deadly
b. rural
c. using very few words
d. very overweight

21. Impetus
a. lacking power
b. regret
c. shamelessness
d. motivation

22. Prevail
a. to fall ill
b. to pay more than necessary
c. to achieve victory
d. to have foresight

23. podium
a. small town
b. insert worn in a shoe
c. raised platform
d. foot doctor

24. Blatant

a. hidden
b. obvious
c. disgusting
d. very old

25. Inflict

a. to devise
b. to demand
c. to revolt
d. to impose

Vocabulary Practice Test 1 Answer Key

1. C: to explain

2. B: agreement

3. D: yearly

4. A: rare

5. B: to persuade

6. B: to provoke

7. B: to appeal to

8. A: arrogant

9. D: questionable

10. A: unusual

11. B: to give

12. A: contempt

13. C: to force

14. B: celebrated

15. D: to embarrass

16. A: to approve

17. D: tendency

18. D: to surrender

19. A: to drink

20. B: rural

21. D: motivation

22. C: to achieve victory

23. C: raised platform

24. B: obvious

25. D: to impose

Vocabulary Practice Test 2

For each word, choose the answer that contains the word or phrase that is closest in meaning.

1. Universal

    a. everywhere
    b. high quality
    c. related to college
    d. poetry that doesn't rhyme

2. Morbid

    a. lacking excitement
    b. average
    c. horizontal
    d. related to death

3. Malicious

    a. spiteful
    b. good-tasting
    c. delicate
    d. intense

4. Quip

    a. a tool
    b. a medical device
    c. a joke
    d. a kind of flower

5. Subtle

    a. slight
    b. round
    c. plain
    d. outdated

6. Broach

    a. to remove
    b. to ban
    c. to bring up
    d. to twist

7. Aphorism

    a. fable
    b. funny story
    c. proverb
    d. cutting remark

8. Innocuous

    a. causing nausea
    b. harmless
    c. dangerous
    d. mysterious

9. Surreptitious

    a. sneaky
    b. very loud
    c. long and winding
    d. saying the same thing

10. Simulate

    a. to excite
    b. to pretend
    c. to connect
    d. to grow fast

11. Precede

    a. to continue
    b. to come after
    c. to come before
    d. to take place

12. Epitaph

    a. curse word
    b. false sounding apology
    c. inscription on a tombstone
    d. engraved invitation

13. Pretentious

    a. pompous
    b. very large
    c. faint-sounding
    d. round

14. Paradox

    a. a matching pair
    b. a contradiction
    c. a small star
    d. half a light-year

15. Superfluous

    a. gigantic
    b. awesome
    c. unnecessary
    d. filled with joy

16. Valid
   a. butler
   b. powerful
   c. fast
   d. legitimate

17. Jargon
   a. language
   b. container
   c. boundary
   d. painter's toolbox

18. Obstinate
   a. backwards
   b. friendly
   c. stubborn
   d. extremely ill

19. Eloquent
   a. equal on all sides
   b. persuasive
   c. of foreign birth
   d. bent

20. Clandestine
   a. shocking
   b. fatal
   c. wise
   d. secret

21. Colloquial
   a. taking place at college
   b. double-jointed
   c. informal
   d. regrettable

22. Conundrum
   a. maze
   b. short novel
   c. riddle
   d. tall tower

23. Placid
   a. drunk
   b. queasy
   c. perfectly round
   d. peaceful

24. haggle

a. to dispute
b. to shout
c. to fray
d. to swallow

25. taciturn

a. polite
b. rude
c. quiet
d. having many curves

Vocabulary Practice Test 2 Answer Key

1. A: everywhere

2. D: related to death

3. A: spiteful

4. C: a joke

5. A: slight

6. C: to bring up

7. C: proverb

8. B: harmless

9. A: sneaky

10. B: to pretend

11. C: to come before

12. C: inscription on a tombstone

13. A: pompous

14. B: a contradiction

15. C: unnecessary

16. D: legitimate

17. A: language

18. C: stubborn

19. B: persuasive

20. D: secret

21. C: informal

22. C: riddle

23. D: peaceful

24. A: to dispute

25. C: quiet

Vocabulary Practice Test 3

For each word, choose the answer that contains the word or phrase that is closest in meaning.

1. Endorse
   a. to remove
   b. to give
   c. to approve
   d. to accelerate

2. Placate
   a. to fasten
   b. to go away
   c. to soothe
   d. to stare

3. Benevolent
   a. charitable
   b. evil
   c. confused
   d. sad

4. Covert
   a. fast
   b. terrible
   c. hidden
   d. go back

5. Larceny
   a. theft
   b. kindness
   c. humor
   d. resolve

6. Poignant
   a. foul-smelling
   b. deeply moving
   c. perfectly ripe
   d. very tasty

7. Aloof
   a. outgoing
   b. insane
   c. intelligent
   d. detached

46

8. Precedent

a. something that happened before
b. something that is happening right now
c. something that will happen later
d. something that will never happen

9. Profound

a. involving money
b. near-sighted
c. deep
d. circular driveway

10. Analogy

a. tongue twister
b. abbreviation from first letter of words
c. cheap reproduction
d. comparison

11. Mode

a. connecting point
b. tool
c. manner
d. dessert

12. Vehemently

a. passionately
b. weakly
c. shabbily
d. rudely

13. Potent

a. a drink with magic properties
b. powerful
c. sharp-edged
d. danger

14. Animosity

a. possessing four legs
b. hatred
c. sheer joy
d. confusion

15. Appease

a. to turn suddenly
b. to soothe
c. to disappear
d. to meet as a group

16. Contrite

a. brief
b. twisted
c. sorry
d. skillful

17. Obsequious

a. subservient
b. bedridden
c. famous
d. cunning

18. Embezzle

a. to steal
b. to give a refund
c. to keep a promise
d. to stir

19. Facetious

a. slightly overweight
b. feeling faint
c. two-faced
d. humorous

20. Benign

a. to speak ill of someone
b. gentle
c. donate
d. equal to or less than

21. Largesse

a. physical size
b. a small island
c. generosity
d. a musical notation

22. Verify

a. to enlarge
b. to prove
c. to copy
d. to deny

23. Rejoinder

a. something left over
b. someone who quits and rejoins
c. a carpenter's tool
d. a witty reply

24. Tenant

    a. principle or belief
    b. person who rents a house
    c. stubborn
    d. high-strung

25. Solicit

    a. to ask for
    b. to refuse
    c. to arrest
    d. to convict

Vocabulary Practice Test 3 Answer Key

1. C: to approve

2. C: to soothe

3. A: charitable

4. C: hidden

5. A: theft

6. B: deeply moving

7. D: detached

8. A: something that happened before

9. C: deep

10. D: comparison

11. C: manner

12. A: passionately

13: B: powerful

14. B: hatred

15. B: to soothe

16. C: sorry

17. A: subservient

18. A: to steal

19. D: humorous

20. B: gentle

21. C: generosity

22. B: to prove

23. D: a witty reply

24. B: person who rents a house

25. A: to ask for

Vocabulary Practice Test 4

For each word, choose the answer that contains the word or phrase that is closest in meaning.

1. Chronic
   a. painful
   b. bent
   c. colorful
   d. long-lasting

2. Coerce
   a. to lie
   b. to cheat
   c. to swerve
   d. to force

3. Abrasive
   a. extended
   b. coarse
   c. magical
   d. checkered

4. Precocious
   a. very cute
   b. adorable
   c. developing early
   d. devout

5. Candid
   a. hidden
   b. shocking
   c. deceitful
   d. honest

6. Wax
   a. to increase
   b. to decrease
   c. to become old
   d. to drop sharply

7. Fortuitous
   a. lucky
   b. heavy
   c. strongly reinforced
   d. well-protected

51

8. Deter
   a. to change one's driving route
   b. to prevent
   c. to cause
   d. to read between the lines

9. Minute
   a. unable to speak
   b. very tiny
   c. belonging to myself
   d. extremely fragile

10. Revert
   a. to turn upside down
   b. to return to a previous condition
   c. to regard as sacred
   d. to turn inside out

11. Hazardous
   a. healthy
   b. deep
   c. very funny
   d. dangerous

12. Proscribe
   a. to recommend
   b. to read
   c. to forbid
   d. to portray

13. Spurn
   a. to reject
   b. to start a fire
   c. to embrace
   d. to threaten

14. Condone
   a. to tie a ribbon
   b. to allow something
   c. to transfer something
   d. to eat in a hurry

15. Evade
   a. to capture
   b. to avoid
   c. to light up
   d. to expel someone from a group

16. Entice

   a. to frighten
   b. to dislike
   c. to attract
   d. to instigate

17. Contrived

   a. artificial
   b. curved
   d. out of breath
   d. very sorry

18. Deprived

   a. having no conscience
   b. unable to walk on one's own
   c. lacking something essential
   d. very disappointed

19. Hyperbole

   a. a distant star
   b. an animal that burrows
   c. exaggerated language
   d. the peak of a roof

20. Clamor

   a. to curdle
   b. to grab
   c. a tool used with anvil
   d. an uproar

21. Averse

   a. reluctant
   b. rhyming
   c. to move across
   d. divided into halves

22. Belligerent

   a. speaking two languages
   b. devout
   c. unfaithful
   d. hostile

23. Desist

   a. dead
   b. to fight against
   c. to stop
   d. to demand

24. Rotund

    a.   round
    b.   loud
    c.   speaking smoothly
    d.   insightful

25. Wrangle

    a.   to deceive
    b.   to argue
    c.   to volunteer
    d.   to hesitate

Vocabulary Practice Test 4 Answer Key

1. D: long lasting

2. D: to force

3. B: coarse

4. C: developing early

5. D: honest

6. A: to increase

7. A: lucky

8. B: to prevent

9. B: very tiny

10. B: to return to a previous condition

11. D: dangerous

12. C: to forbid

13. A: to reject

14. B: to allow something

15. B: to avoid

16. C: to attract

17. A: artificial

18. C: lacking something essential

19. C: exaggerated language

20. D: an uproar

21. A: reluctant

22. D: hostile

23. C: to stop

24. A: round

25. B: to argue

Analogies

Another kind of language question you might see is one asking you to draw an analogy, and this kind of question is different from the other kinds we've already discussed. Instead, you'll see something like this:

1. Mare : Foal
    a. Dog : Cat
    b. Dolphin : Tuna
    c. Shark : Whale
    d. Hen : Chick

You're looking for two words that have the same relationship as the two words in the question stem. Here's what a full analogy looks like:

Food: Plate :: Beverage : Glass

Here is what the analogy means:

Food is to plate as beverage is to glass.

In other words, a beverage has the same relationship to a glass as food has to a plate. In both cases, the second item is used to serve the first item.

In the example above, select the answer that contains two words with the same kind of relationship as *mare* and *foal*. While all the pairs in the answers have some similarities, only *d* contains the same relationship of an adult female and a young animal of the same species.

Don't let analogy questions intimidate you. Just think of them exactly as they are—another kind of vocabulary question. In fact, some will be nothing more than synonym/antonym questions. If you've never answered analogy questions before, they might seem tricky, but once you've gone through a few of our practice questions, you'll see they're really nothing to worry about.

Sometimes the analogy questions have a slightly different format. For example, you might see a question phrased like this:

Mare : Foal :: Hen :
    a. rooster
    b. duck
    c. chick
    d. goose

As you can see, completing these kinds of analogies isn't much different than the first format; in fact, this layout may be a bit easier since you're given more information to start with.

One thing to keep in mind is that the order of the words is extremely important. The two words in the correct answer must not only have the same relationship as the two words in the question stem, they must also be in the same order. Mare : Foal :: Hen : Chick is correct because a mare is an adult female horse and a foal is a young horse, while a hen is an adult female chicken and a chick is a young chicken. However, Chick : Hen would *not* be a correct answer, because even though both elements of the analogy are present, they are in reverse order, changing the relationship.

56

Analogies can represent many different kinds of relationships. Here are some of the most common:

- Synonyms—question : query
- Antonyms—straight : meandering
- Whole/Part—finger : hand | foot : toe
- Classification/Kind/Category/Composition, etc.—owl : nocturnal | owl : bird | building : brick | red : color | apparel : shirt
- Single/Group—cow : herd | tree : forest
- Degree—big : huge | angry : furious | tired : exhausted | hot : warm
- Subject/Action—doctor : prescribe | attorney : defend
- Action/Subject—hit : ball | levy : tax
- Object/User—wrench : mechanic | conductor : baton
- Object/Place—flower : garden | office : desk
- Object/Action—pen : write | cut : knife
- Cause/Effect—virus : illness | practice : improvement | stress : anxiety
- Aspect—cheetah : fast | mansion : huge

These are some of the most common kinds of analogies found on civil service exams. There are others, but there's no need to cover every conceivable kind of analogy you might run into. Ninety percent of the analogies you'll see will fall into one of the above categories, and you should have no trouble spotting the relationship in any that don't. Use the practice questions in this guide, as they can help you tremendously if you're having any trouble in this area.

Analogies Practice Test 1

Directions: For each of the following questions, you will find three capitalized terms and, in parentheses, four answer choices designated a, b, c, and d. Select the one answer choice that best completes the analogy with the three capitalized terms. (To record your answers, circle your answer choice.)

1. CHASTISE : REPRIMAND :: IMPETUOUS : _____

    a. punish
    b. rash
    c. considered
    d. poor

2. TELE : DISTANT :: CIRCUM : _____

    a. through
    b. above
    c. within
    d. around

3. CHENEY: BUSH :: MONDALE : _____

    a. Clinton
    b. Carter
    c. Reagan
    d. Obama

4. LISSOM : GRACEFUL :: _____ : OBSTREPEROUS

    a. hostile
    b. lithe
    c. determined
    d. unconditional

5. HUMERUS : ARM :: _____ : OBSTREPEROUS : LEG

    a. ulna
    b. clavicle
    c. femur
    d. mandible

6. PRODUCT : _____ :: MULTIPLICATION : DIVISION

    a. quotient
    b. divisor
    c. integer
    d. dividend

7. SWEATER : _____ :: WEAR : EAT

    a. shirt
    b. top hat
    c. asparagus
    d. looks

8. IMPECUNIOUS : MONEY :: _____ : FOOD

    a. famished
    b. nauseated
    c. distracted
    d. antagonistic

9. DENIGRATE : MALIGN :: DEMUR : _____

    a. protest
    b. defer
    c. slander
    d. benumb

10. POST : AFTER :: PERI : _____

    a. around
    b. completely
    c. before
    d. much

11. GOAT : NANNY :: PIG : _____

    a. shoat
    b. ewe
    c. cub
    d. sow

12. CACHE : RESERVE :: DEARTH : _____

    a. stockpile
    b. paucity
    c. cudgel
    d. dirge

13. DISCURSIVE : DIGRESSIVE :: SUCCINCT : _____

    a. long-winded
    b. pithy
    c. taciturn
    d. staccato

14. ARABLE : FARMABLE :: ASYLUM : _____

    a. refuge
    b. danger
    c. arid
    d. fertile

15. SATIRE : HUMOR :: BUREAU : _____

    a. bureaucracy
    b. furniture
    c. complaint
    d. bedroom

16. TITAN : GIANT :: PROGENITOR : _____

    a. forebear
    b. descendant
    c. miniature
    d. primeval

17. MYRIAD : STATIONARY :: FEW : _____

    a. peripatetic
    b. many
    c. several
    d. halted

18. ZENITH : NADIR :: _____ : DISOBEDIENT

    a. defiant
    b. apex
    c. grandiloquent
    d. tractable

19. MISSISSIPPI : UNITED STATES :: THAMES : _____

    a. France
    b. England
    c. Germany
    d. Belgium

20. MANSION : HOUSE :: _____ : BOTTLE

    a. flagon
    b. container
    c. vessel
    d. pot

21. DICTIONARY : DEFINITIONS :: THESAURUS : _____

    a. pronunciations
    b. synonyms
    c. explanations
    d. pronouns

22. BEES : HIVE :: CATTLE : _____

    a. swarm
    b. pod
    c. herd
    d. flock

23. DIRGE : LAMENT :: PURGE : _____

    a. elegy
    b. weeping
    c. cleanse
    d. limpid

24. LATITUDE : LONGITUDE : PARALLEL : _____

a. strait
b. meridian
c. equator
d. aquifer

25. WIT : WAG :: INSOLENCE : _____

a. boor
b. student
c. teacher
d. soldier

26. PREVENTION : DETERRENCE :: INCITEMENT : _____

a. excitement
b. provocation
c. request
d. disregard

27. ARCH : SAUCY :: _____ : ENMITY

a. antipathy
b. oval
c. circular
d. delectable

28. NOISOME : _____ :: THUNDEROUS : DEAFENING

a. pleasant
b. boisterous
c. malodorous
d. silent

29. INFIDEL : UNBELIEVER :: _____ : OUTCAST

a. pariah
b. apostate
c. apostle
d. disciple

30. VALUE : WORTH :: MEASURE : _____

a. gauge
b. allowance
c. demerit
d. insignificance

31. DOLPHIN : POD :: GOOSE : _____

a. troup
b. nest
c. gaggle
d. drove

61

32. DISSEMINATE : SPREAD :: DEPRECATE : _____

    a. disparage
    b. demur
    c. dispel
    d. dissemble

33. EGO : CONSCIOUS :: _____ : UNCONSCIOUS

    a. operant
    b. id
    c. identity
    d. collective

34. MAL : _____ :: NEO : NEW

    a. water
    b. bad
    c. change
    d. hand

35. PEDOLOGY : CHILDREN :: ICHTHYOLOGY : _____

    a. insects
    b. fishes
    c. ants
    d. fungi

36. BLITHE : CAREFREE :: BRUSQUE : _____

    a. curt
    b. civil
    c. urbane
    d. courteous

37. SONNET : 14 :: HAIKU : _____

    a. 3
    b. 5.
    c. 7
    d. 9

38. WOLF : WOLVES :: PASSERBY : _____

    a. passerby
    b. passerbys
    c. passersby
    d. passersbys

39. CANDID : FRANK :: CAPITULATE : _____

    a. repeat
    b. surrender
    c. burnish
    d. chapter

40. BEAR : DONKEY :: CUB : _____

    a. kid
    b. pup
    c. foal
    d. joey

41. MOLLUSK : SNAIL :: MARSUPIAL : _____

    a. koala
    b. mouse
    c. raccoon
    d. squirrel

42. DEARTH : PAUCITY :: COUNTENANCE : _____

    a. condone
    b. deny
    c. express
    d. cower

43. DEER : FAWN :: LION : _____

    a. kid
    b. cub
    c. cygnet
    d. shoat

44. LUCRE : PROFIT :: OFFICIOUS : _____

    a. bureaucratic
    b. meddling
    c. authoritarian
    d. legal

45. CARPE DIEM : SEIZE THE DAY :: PERSONA NON GRATA : _____

    a. ungrateful person
    b. unwelcome person
    c. absent person
    d. anonymous person

46. ALACRITY : LASSITUDE :: ANTIPATHY : _____

    a. dislike
    b. hatred
    c. sympathy
    d. beneficence

47. LOCK : PRIDE :: _____ : LIONS

    a. key
    b. permit
    c. collection
    d. hair

48. ENERVATE : ENERGIZE :: ESPOUSE : _____

a. oppose
b. wed
c. equine
d. epistolary

49. CHERUB : CHERUBIM :: NEBULA : _____

a. nebuli
b. nebulae
c. nebulus
d. nebulous

50. DIATRIBE : DIALECT :: JEREMIAD : _____

a. eject
b. tirade
c. mermaid
d. idiom

51. SOPRANO : FEMALE :: _____ : MALE

a. tenor
b. alto
c. bass
d. contralto

52. GENUS : GENERA :: ALUMNUS : _____

a. alumni
b. alumna
c. alumnae
d. alum

53. HISS : OR :: ONOMATOPOEIA : _____

a. preposition
b. verb
c. pronoun
d. conjunction

54. PROSCRIBE : PRESCRIBE :: DENOUNCE : _____

a. dictate
b. repel
c. invite
d. dentition

55. EWE : _____ :: MARE : HORSE

a. sheep
b. goat
c. lamb
d. cow

56. XCIV : 94 :: XXXVI : _____

    a. 106
    b. 136
    c. 134
    d. 36

57. INUNDATE : FLOOD :: JARGON : _____

    a. argot
    b. language
    c. precipitation
    d. overwhelm

58. 8 : 2 :: 64 : _____

    a. 2
    b. 4
    c. 8
    d. 12

59. HER : ME :: _____ : FIRST

    a. first
    b. second
    c. third
    d. fourth

60. SCORE: GROSS :: 20 : _____

    a. 1
    b. 5
    c. 15
    d. 144

Analogies Practice Test 1 Answers and Explanations

1. B: Rash. Chastise and reprimand are synonyms. Rash is a synonym for impulsive.

2. D: Around. As the prefix tele- means distant, the prefix circa- means around.

3. B: Carter. As Cheney was US Vice President in President Bush's administration, so Mondale was in President Carter's administration.

4. A: Hostile. Lissom and graceful are synonyms. The answer choice synonym for obstreperous is hostile.

5. C: Femur. The humerus is a bone in the arm; the femur is a bone in the leg.

6. A: Quotient. A quotient is the result of division as a product is the result of multiplication.

7. C: Asparagus. One eats asparagus; one wears a sweater.

8. A: Famished. As a person who is impecunious needs money, so a person who is famished needs food.

9. A: Protest. Denigrate and malign are synonyms. The answer choice synonym for demur is protest.

10. A: Around. As the prefix post- means after, the prefix peri- means around.

11. D: Sow. A female goat is a nanny and a female pig is a sow.

12. B: Paucity. Cache and reserve are synonyms. The answer choice synonym for dearth is paucity.

13. B: Pithy. Discursive and digressive are synonyms. The answer choice synonym for succinct is pithy.

14. A: Refuge. Arable and farmable are synonyms. The answer choice synonym for asylum is refuge.

15. B: Furniture. Satire is a kind of humor and a bureau is a kind of furniture.

16. A: Forebear. Titan and Giant are synonyms. The answer choice synonym for progenitor is forebear.

17. A: Peripatetic. Myriad and few are antonyms. The answer choice antonym for stationary is peripatetic.

18. D: Tractable. Zenith and nadir are antonyms. The answer choice antonym for disobedient is tractable.

19. B: England. As the Mississippi is a river in the United States, so the Thames is a river in England.

20. A: Flagon. As a mansion is a large house, so a flagon is a large bottle.

66

21. B: Synonyms. As a dictionary is a collection of definitions, so a thesaurus is a collection of synonyms.

22. C: Herd. A group of bees is called a hive and a group of cattle is called a herd.

23. C: Cleanse. Dirge and lament are synonyms. The answer choice synonym for purge is cleanse.

24. B: Meridian. A parallel is a line of latitude, while a meridian is a ling of longitude.

25. A: Boor. A defining quality of a wag is wit, as a defining quality of a boor is insolence.

26. B: Provocation. Prevention and deterrence are synonyms. The answer choice synonym for incitement is provocation.

27. A: Antipathy. Arch and saucy are synonyms. The answer choice synonym for enmity is antipathy.

28. C: Malodorous. Thunderous and deafening are synonyms. The answer choice synonym for noisome is malodorous.

29. A: Pariah. As an unbeliever with respect to a particular religion is called an infidel, so an outcast is called a pariah (in Hindu castes).

30. A: Gauge. Value and worth are synonyms. The answer choice synonym for measure is gauge.

31. C: Gaggle. A group of dolphins is called a pod and a group of geese is called a gaggle.

32. A: Disparage. Disseminate and spread are synonyms. The answer choice synonym for deprecate is disparage.

33. B: Id. In Freudian theory the ego is the conscious component of the psyche and the id is the unconscious component of the psyche.

34. B: Bad. As the prefix neo- means new, the prefix mal- means bad.

35. B: Fishes. As pedology is the study of children, so ichthyology is the study of fishes.

36. A: Curt. Blithe and carefree are synonyms. The answer choice synonym for brusque is curt.

37. A: 3. In poetry, a sonnet has 14 lines and a haiku has 3 lines.

38. C: Passersby. The plural of wolf is wolves and the plural of passerby is passersby.

39. B: Surrender. Candid and frank are synonyms. The answer choice synonym for capitulate is surrender.

40. C: Foal. As a bear baby is called a cub, so a donkey baby is called a foal.

41. A: Koala. A snail is an example of a mollusk and a koala is an example of a marsupial.

42. A: Condone. Dearth and paucity are synonyms. The answer choice synonym for countenance is condone.

43. B: Cub. As a deer's offspring is called a fawn, so a lion's offspring is called a cub.

44. B: Meddling. Lucre and profit are synonyms. The answer choice synonym for officious is meddling.

45. B: Unwelcome person. As carpe diem means seize the day, so persona non grata means unwelcome person.

46. C: Sympathy. Alacrity and lassitude are antonyms. The answer choice antonym for antipathy is sympathy.

47. D: Hair. The collective noun for lions is a pride; the collective noun for hair is a lock.

48. A: Oppose. Enervate and energize are antonyms. The answer choice antonym for espouse is oppose.

49. B: Nebulae. As the plural of cherub is cherubim, so the plural of nebula is nebulae.

50. D: Idiom. Diatribe and jeremiad are synonyms. The answer choice synonym for dialect is idiom.

51. A: Tenor. As soprano is the highest female vocal range, tenor is the highest adult male vocal range.

52. A: Alumni. Alumni is the plural form of alumnus as genera is the plural form of genus.

53. D: Conjunction. Or is an example of a conjunction as hiss is an example of onomatopoeia.

54. A: Dictate. Proscribe and denounce are synonyms. The answer choice synonym for prescribe is dictate.

55. A: Sheep. A ewe is a female sheep as a mare is a female horse.

56. D: 36. As XCIV is the Roman numeral representation of 94, so XXXVI is the Roman numeral representation of 36.

57. A: Argot. Inundate and flood are synonyms. The answer choice synonym for jargon is argot.

58. B: 4. 8 squared is 64. 2 squared is 4.

59. C: Third. Her is a third-person pronoun and me is a first-person pronoun.

60. D: 144. As a score is 20, so a gross is 144.

Analogies Practice Test 2

Directions: For each of the following questions, you will find three capitalized terms and, in parentheses, four answer choices designated a, b, c, and d. Select the one answer choice that best completes the analogy with the three capitalized terms. To record your answers, circle your answer choice.

1. AUSPICIOUS : OMINOUS :: PARSIMONIOUS : _____
   a. spendthrift
   b. frugal
   c. licentious
   d. secular

2. ORATOR : ELOQUENCE :: PESSIMIST : _____
   a. fluency
   b. naysayer
   c. hopelessness
   d. thoughtfulness

3. CONTUMACIOUS : INSUBORDINATE :: DIATRIBE : _____
   a. obedient
   b. indirect
   c. suppress
   d. tirade

4. AD HOC: COMMITTEE :: _____ : FABRIC
   a. chenille
   b. extemporized
   c. composition
   d. propaganda

5. TWAIN : CLEMENS :: CARROLL : _____
   a. Dodgson
   b. squally
   c. Lewis
   d. thrice

6. COLORADO : CO :: MARYLAND : _____
   a. MA
   b. MD
   c. MR
   d. ML

7. INTER : BETWEEN :: TRANS : _____
   a. above
   b. without
   c. within
   d. across

69

8. PERSPICACIOUS : DENSE :: _____ : INSIPID
   a. thrilling
   b. boring
   c. intuitive
   d. uninspired

9. VERB : COLLATE :: PREPOSITION : _____
   a. the
   b. behind
   c. used
   d. perfectly

10. MEET : _____ :: SATE : APPETITE
   a. need
   b. whim
   c. option
   d. companion

11. CIRCLE : CIRCUMFERENCE :: OCTAGON : _____
   a. area
   b. perimeter
   c. radius
   d. width

12. _____ : RED :: KELLY : GREEN
   a. king
   b. tide
   c. grace
   d. crimson

13. BERET : _____ :: HAT : SHOE
   a. alpine
   b. balaclava
   c. wingtip
   d. bonnet

14. MANE : _____ :: CANE : KEN
   a. knowledge
   b. stick
   c. hair
   d. men

15. ABACUS : CALCULATOR :: MIMEOGRAPH : _____
   a. fax machine
   b. word processor
   c. photocopier
   d. telegraph

16. CLANDESTINE : SURREPTITIOUS :: COGENT : _____

    a. incoherent
    b. persuasive
    c. secretive
    d. officious

17. CRANIUM : HEAD :: _____ : ARM

    a. femur
    b. clavicle
    c. ulna
    d. sternum

18. ASHEN : WHITE :: _____ : RED

    a. octave
    b. sanguine
    c. ermine
    d. mauve

19. BELLICOSE : WAR :: BACCHANALIAN : _____

    a. party
    b. solitude
    c. outdoors
    d. luxury

20. SOBRIQUET : ALIAS :: STOLID : _____

    a. pseudonym
    b. solid
    c. impassive
    d. tourniquet

21. PANTS : WEAR :: CHAMPAGNE : _____

    a. eat
    b. dress
    c. drink
    d. applaud

22. COMPARATIVE : MORE :: SUPERLATIVE : _____

    a. some
    b. more
    c. all
    d. most

23. AXIS : ITALY :: ALLIES : _____

    a. Japan
    b. Germany
    c. England
    d. Spain

24. NEPHOLOGY : PATHOLOGY :: _____ : DISEASES

a. Egypt
b. archaeology
c. parasites
d. clouds

25. ILK : ELK :: BIG : _____

a. moose
b. type
c. beg
d. enormous

26. HUSBAND : ECONOMIZE :: MARRY : _____

a. wife
b. save
c. spouse
d. unite

27. SEDATIVE : SLEEPINESS :: ALCOHOL : _____

a. intoxication
b. anger
c. thirst
d. solitude

28. BASS : MALE :: _____ : FEMALE

a. alto
b. contralto
c. soprano
d. tenor

29. ISOSCELES : SCALENE :: RECTANGLE : _____

a. circle
b. square
c. geometry
d. octagon

30. INVETERATE : HABITUAL :: QUOTIDIAN : _____

a. numerical
b. commonplace
c. absolute
d. vertebrate

31. SON-IN-LAW : SONS-IN-LAW :: THESIS : _____

a. thesi
b. theses
c. thesises
d. theseses

32. TABULA RASA : BLANK SLATE :: SUI GENERIS : _____

    a. indispensible

    b. appropriate

    c. one of a kind

    d. no contest

33. ARACHNOPHOBIA : SPIDERS :: _____ : HEIGHTS

    a. acrophobia

    b. agoraphobia

    c. latiphobia

    d. longiphobia

34. FRENETIC : _____ :: FEVERISH : GUILE

    a. ingenuous

    b. duplicity

    c. toil

    d. turmoil

35. GENUS : HOMO :: SPECIES : _____

    a. sapiens

    b. animalia

    c. chordate

    d. hominidae

36. DEBILITATE : INVIGORATE :: DIFFIDENT : _____

    a. shy

    b. energize

    c. brash

    d. similar

37. GROVEL : ASK :: DEMAND : _____

    a. consider

    b. ponder

    c. request

    d. refuse

38. CLOY : SATIATE :: DAUNTLESS : _____

    a. needy

    b. fearless

    c. contentious

    d. deleterious

39. EFFERVESCENT : LIVELY :: EFFETE : _____

    a. fair

    b. faithful

    c. bubbly

    d. exhausted

40. VENERATE : HONOR :: UNDULATE : _____

   a. obey
   b. withstand
   c. fluctuate
   d. ingratiate

41. RIPOSTE : RETORT :: MELANGE : _____

   a. question
   b. mixture
   c. request
   d. melody

42. HERETICAL : HETERODOX :: _____ : ILLICIT

   a. unlawful
   b. legitimate
   c. spoken
   d. illusory

43. KABUL : AFGHANISTAN :: _____ : CANADA

   a. Quebec
   b. Vancouver
   c. Ottawa
   d. Toronto

44. PERIODICAL : MAGAZINE :: OCCASIONAL : _____

   a. always
   b. novel
   c. intermittent
   d. never

45. NOUN : DEDICATION :: VERB : _____

   a. dedicate
   b. deed
   c. from
   d. decision

46. NIMBUS : CLOUD :: IGUANA : _____

   a. green
   b. hard
   c. lizard
   d. cirrus

47. ADAPT : ADEPT :: CHANGE : _____

   a. skilled
   b. changed
   c. changeable
   d. inapt

48. ALFRESCO : OUTDOORS :: DE RIGUEUR : _____

a. rigid
b. necessary
c. retaliatory
d. haughty

49. IMPASSIVE : EXPRESSIVE :: LOQUACIOUS : _____

a. taciturn
b. garrulous
c. aloof
d. permeable

50. 1/6 : 7/12 :: 6 : _____

a. 3
b. 7
c. 21
d. 30

51. AMERICAN REVOLUTION : BUNKER HILL :: AMERICAN CIVIL WAR : _____

a. Valley Forge
b. Antietam
c. Dunkirk
d. Marne

52. BEAR : _____ :: LION : LEONINE

a. ursine
b. bovine
c. porcine
d. ovine

53. MORSE : CODE :: BELL : _____

a. phonograph
b. telephone
c. fire engine
d. jingle

54. BLANDISH : BRANDISH :: CAJOLE : _____

a. wield
b. praise
c. Cajun
d. decline

55. BOVINE : COW :: EQUINE : _____

a. equality
b. horse
c. fox
d. vulture

56. BROACH : RAISE :: BROOCH : _____

    a. rise
    b. ornamental pin
    c. raisin
    d. stick

57. BUCOLIC : COUNTRY :: URBAN : _____

    a. village
    b. state
    c. city
    d. built-up

58. TREASON : TRAITOR :: MURDER : _____

    a. murderous
    b. autocrat
    c. brazen
    d. felon

59. AMELIORATE : BETTER :: ADULTERATE : _____

    a. impure
    b. mediocre
    c. ambulatory
    d. ambivalent

60. ADMIRE : ADORE :: DISLIKE : _____

    a. discomfit
    b. detest
    c. antipathy
    d. horror

Analogies Practice Test 2 Answers and Explanations

1. A: Spendthrift. Auspicious and ominous are antonyms. The answer choice antonym for parsimonious is spendthrift.

2. C: Hopelessness. A characteristic quality of an orator is eloquence; a characteristic quality of a pessimist is hopelessness.

3. D: Tirade. Contumacious and insubordinate are synonyms. The answer choice synonym for diatribe is tirade.

4. A: Chenille. As chenille is a type of fabric, so Ad Hoc is a type of committee.

5. A: Dodgson. The author Samuel Clemens used the pseudonym Mark Twain, as the author Charles Dodgson used the pseudonym Lewis Carroll.

6. B: MD. As the postal code for Colorado is CO, the postal code for Maryland is MD.

7. D: Across. As the prefix inter- means between, the prefix trans- means across.

8. A: Thrilling. Perspicacious and dense are antonyms. The answer choice antonym for insipid is thrilling.

9. B: Behind. Collate is an example of a verb; behind is an example of a preposition.

10. A: Need. To meet a need is to satisfy it, and to sate an appetite is to satisfy it.

11. B: Perimeter. As the circumference is the measurement of the outer boundary of a circle, the perimeter is the measurement of the outer boundary of an octagon.

12. D: Crimson. As kelly is a shade of green, so is crimson a shade of red.

13. C: Wingtip. A wingtip is a type of shoe as a beret is a type of hat.

14. D: Men. As mane rhymes with cane, so men rhymes with ken.

15. C: Photocopier. An abacus was an early technology that served some of the same functions as a calculator does today; similarly, a mimeograph was an early technology that served some of the same functions that a photocopier serves today.

16. B: Persuasive. Clandestine and surreptitious are synonyms. The answer choice synonym for cogent is persuasive.

17. C: Ulna. The cranium is in the head and the ulna is in the arm.

18. B: Sanguine. Ashen describes a color closest to white; sanguine describes a shade of red.

19. A: Party. Someone who is bellicose is drawn to war as someone who is bacchanalian is drawn to parties.

Mometrix

20. C: Impassive. Sobriquet and alias are synonyms. The answer choice synonym for stolid is impassive.

21. C: Drink. As one drinks champagne, so one wears pants.

22. D: Most. More is the comparative form measuring quantity, and most is the superlative form.

23. C: England. England was one of the Allies during World War II as Italy was one of the Axis nations.

24. D: Clouds. Nephology is the study of clouds as pathology is the study of diseases.

25. C: Beg. If you replace the vowel in ilk with an e, you get elk. Similarly, if you replace the vowel in big with an e, you get beg.

26. D: Unite. Husband and economize are synonyms. The answer choice synonym for marry is unite.

27. A: Intoxication. As ingesting a sedative leads to sleepiness, so ingesting alcohol leads to intoxication.

28. B: Contralto. As bass is the lowest male vocal range, so contralto is the lowest female vocal range.

29. B: Square. Isosceles and scalene are both types of triangles, as rectangles and squares are both types of quadrilaterals.

30. B: Commonplace. Inveterate and habitual are synonyms. The answer choice synonym for quotidian is commonplace.

31. B: Theses. As the plural of son-in-law is sons-in-law, so the plural of thesis is theses.

32. C: One of a kind. As tabula rasa means a blank slate, so sui generis means one of a kind.

33. A: Acrophobia. As arachnophobia is the fear of spiders, so acrophobia is the fear of heights.

34. B: Duplicity. Frenetic and feverish are synonyms. The answer choice synonym for guile is duplicity.

35. A: Sapiens. Homo is an example of a genus, while sapiens is an example of a species.

36. C: Brash. Debilitate and invigorate are antonyms. The answer choice antonym for diffident is brash.

37. C: Request. Grovel is an extreme way to ask; demand is an extreme way to request.

38. B: Fearless. Cloy and satiate are synonyms. The answer choice synonym for dauntless is fearless.

39. D: Exhausted. Effervescent and lively are synonyms. The answer choice synonym for effete is exhausted.

40. C: Fluctuate. Venerate and honor are synonyms. The answer choice synonym for undulate is fluctuate.

Mømetrix

41. B: Mixture. Riposte means retort and mélange means mixture.

42. A: Unlawful. Heretical and heterodox are synonyms. The answer choice synonym for illicit is unlawful.

43. C: Ottawa. As Kabul is the capital of Afghanistan, so is Ottawa the capital of Canada.

44. C: Intermittent. Periodical and magazine are synonyms. The answer choice synonym for occasional is intermittent. Although periodical could also be a synonym for occasional, there is no synonym for magazine among the answer choices.

45. A: Dedicate. Dedication is a noun and dedicate is a verb.

46. C: Lizard. As a nimbus is a type of cloud, so an iguana is a type of lizard.

47. A: Skilled. As adapt means change, so adept means skilled.

48. B: Necessary. As al fresco means outdoors, so de rigueur means necessary.

49. A: Taciturn. Impassive and expressive are antonyms. The answer choice antonym for loquacious is taciturn.

50. C: 21. The fractions 1/6 and 7/12 have a ratio of 1 to 3.5 as do the integers 6 and 21. (Multiply 1/6 by 7/2 to get 7/12; multiply 6 by 7/2 to get 21.)

51. B: Antietam. Antietam was a major battle of the American Civil War as Bunker Hill was a major battle of the American Revolution.

52. A: Ursine. As leonine refers to lions, so ursine refers to bears.

53. B: Telephone. As Samuel Morse is known for his invention of Morse code, so Alexander Graham Bell is known for his invention of the telephone.

54. A: Wield. Blandish and cajole are synonyms. The answer choice synonym for brandish is wield.

55. B: Horse. As bovine refers to cows, so equine refers to horses.

56. B: Ornamental pin. Broach and raise are synonyms. The answer choice synonym for brooch is ornamental pin.

57. C: City. Bucolic is a term to describe the country as urban is a term to describe the city.

58. D: Felon. One who commits murder is a felon as one who commits treason is a traitor.

59. A: Impure. When something is ameliorated it is made better; when something is adulterated it is made impure.

60. B: Detest. To detest someone is to dislike him/her extremely, as to adore someone is to admire him/her extremely.

79

Copyright © Mometrix Media. You have been licensed one copy of this document for personal use only. Any other reproduction or redistribution is strictly prohibited. All rights reserved.

Reading Comprehension

There are many kinds of civil service jobs, but one thing they all have in common is reading. Every civil service job in existence requires at least some reading on a regular basis, even if it's only reading forms that need to be filled out, along with the occasional memo. Many jobs, however, will involve extensive, frequent reading. In fact, the amount of reading required in most civil service positions is substantial. That's why reading comprehension is one of the most important topics covered on most exams for these careers.

You'll need to be able to read at an acceptable speed while also being able to clearly understand what you've read. The ability to follow instructions is essential for civil service careers, and in most cases, you'll be given written instructions. Not all of them will be simple and clear cut. In many situations the directions (or any other written material you'll be working with) will require you to do one thing in one kind of situation, do something else in another situation, and take yet another action in a third scenario. It's likely that you'll be expected to make important decisions based on material you've read. A person who is always asking coworkers or supervisors for clarification of written orders and memos will not be a very productive employee. He/she will also be a drag on the productivity of others, which is not acceptable.

If reading is not your strong suit, you'll want to remedy that before sitting down and taking the civil service exam. Without strong reading comprehension skills, it's going to be virtually impossible to get a high enough score to qualify for a job. Even if a person manages to get hired despite poor reading skills, he'll find that it will be very difficult to succeed on the job, or even enjoy going to work. If you need improvement in this area, you'll want to start working on it right away. Improving your reading skills can be done, and you can achieve remarkable results if you're diligent and willing to work hard, but it takes time. It can't be accomplished overnight. This guide will give you knowledge you need to improve your reading comprehension and exercises to help measure your progress.

IMPORTANT SKILLS

TOPICS AND MAIN IDEAS

One of the most important skills in reading comprehension is the identification of topics and main ideas. There is a subtle difference between the two. The topic is the subject of a text, or what the text is about. The main idea, on the other hand, is the most important point being made by the author. The topic is usually expressed in a few words at the most, while the main idea often needs a full sentence to be completely defined. As an example, a short passage might have the topic of penguins and the main idea *Penguins are different from other birds in many ways*. In most nonfiction writing, the topic and the main idea will be stated directly, often in a sentence at the very beginning or end of the text. When being tested on an understanding of the author's topic, the reader can quickly *skim* the passage for the general idea, stopping to read only the first sentence of each paragraph. A paragraph's first sentence is often (though not always) the main topic sentence, and it gives you a summary of the content of the paragraph. However, there are cases in which the reader must figure out an unstated topic or main idea. In these instances, the student must read every sentence of the text and come up with an overarching idea that is supported by each of those sentences.

SUPPORTING DETAILS

While the main idea is the overall premise of a story, supporting details provide evidence and backing for the main point. In order to show that a main idea is correct, or valid, the author needs to add details that prove the point. All texts contain details, but they are only classified as supporting details when they serve to reinforce some larger point. Supporting details are most commonly found in informative and persuasive texts. In some cases, they will be clearly indicated with words like *for example* or *for instance*, or they will be enumerated with words like *first*, *second*, and *last*. However, they are not always indicated with special words. As a reader, it is important to consider whether the author's supporting details really back up the main point. Supporting details can be factual and correct but still not relevant to the author's point. Conversely, supporting details can seem pertinent but be ineffective because they are based on opinion or assertions that cannot be proven.

An example of a main idea is: "Giraffes live in the Serengeti of Africa." A supporting detail about giraffes could be: "A giraffe uses its long neck to reach twigs and leaves on trees." The main idea gives the general idea that the text is about giraffes. The supporting detail gives a specific fact about how the giraffes eat.

> **Review Video: Supporting Details**
> Visit mometrix.com/academy and enter code: 396297

THEME

As opposed to a main idea, themes are seldom expressed directly in a text, so they can be difficult to identify. A theme is an issue, idea, or question raised by the text. For instance, a theme of Shakespeare's *Hamlet* is indecision, as the title character explores his own psyche and the results of his failure to make bold choices. A great work of literature may have many themes, and the reader is justified in identifying any for which he or she can find support. One common characteristic of themes is that they raise more questions than they answer. In a good piece of fiction, the author is not always trying to convince the reader, but is instead trying to elevate the reader's perspective and encourage him to consider the themes more deeply. When reading, one can identify themes by constantly asking what general issues the text is addressing. A good way to evaluate an author's approach to a theme is to begin reading with a question in mind (for example, how does this text approach the theme of love?) and then look for textual evidence that addresses that question.

PURPOSES FOR WRITING

POSITION

In order to be an effective reader, one must pay attention to the author's position and purpose. Even texts that seem objective and impartial, like textbooks, have a position and bias. Readers need to take these into account when considering the author's message. When an author uses emotional language or clearly favors one side of an argument, his position is clear. However, the author's position may be evident not only in what he writes, but in what he doesn't write. For this reason, it is sometimes necessary to review other texts on the same topic in order to understand the author's position. If this is not possible, it may be useful to acquire a little background personal information about the author. When the only source of information is the text, however, the reader should look for language and argumentation that seems to indicate a particular stance on the subject.

> **Review Video: Author's Position**
> Visit mometrix.com/academy and enter code: 827954

PURPOSE

Identifying the purpose of an author is usually easier than identifying her position. In most cases, the author has no interest in hiding his or her purpose. A text that is meant to entertain, for instance, should be obviously written to please the reader. Most narratives, or stories, are written to entertain, though they may also inform or persuade. Informative texts are easy to identify as well. The most difficult purpose to identify is persuasion, because the author has an interest in making this purpose hard to detect. When a person knows that the author is trying to convince him, he is automatically more wary and skeptical of the argument. For this reason, persuasive texts often try to establish an entertaining tone, hoping to amuse the reader into agreement, or an informative tone, hoping to create an appearance of authority and objectivity.

An author's purpose is often evident in the organization of the text. For instance, if the text has headings and subheadings, if key terms are in bold, and if the author makes his main idea clear from the beginning, then the likely purpose of the text is to inform. If the author begins by making a claim and then makes various arguments to support that claim, the purpose is probably to persuade. If the author is telling a story, or is more interested in holding the attention of the reader than in making a particular point or delivering information, then his purpose is most likely to entertain. As a reader, it is best to judge an author on how well he accomplishes his purpose. In other words, it is not entirely fair to complain that a textbook is boring: if the text is clear and easy to understand, then the author has done his job. Similarly, a storyteller should not be judged too harshly for slightly altering a fact to fit his story, so long as he is able to entertain the reader.

PERSUASIVE ESSAY

The author's purpose for writing will affect both his writing style and the reader's response. In a persuasive essay, the author is attempting to change the reader's mind or convince him of something he did not believe previously. There are several identifying characteristics of persuasive writing. One is opinion presented as fact. When an author attempts to persuade the reader, he often presents his or her opinions as if they were fact. A reader must be on guard for statements that sound factual but cannot be subjected to research, observation, or experimentation. Another characteristic of persuasive writing is emotional language. An author will often try to play on the reader's emotion by appealing to his sympathy or sense of morality. When an author uses colorful or evocative language with the intent of arousing the reader's passions, it is likely that he is attempting to persuade. Finally, in many cases a persuasive text will give an unfair explanation of opposing positions, if these positions are mentioned at all.

INFORMATIVE TEXT

An informative text is written to educate and enlighten the reader. Informative texts are almost always nonfiction, and are rarely structured as a story. The intention of an informative text is to deliver information in the most comprehensible way possible, so the structure of the text is likely to be very clear. In an informative text, the thesis statement is often in the first sentence. The author may use descriptive language, but is likely to put more emphasis on clarity and precision. Informative essays do not typically appeal to the emotions. They often contain facts and figures, and rarely include the opinion of the author. Sometimes a persuasive essay can resemble an informative essay, especially if the author maintains an even tone and presents his or her views as if they were established fact.

> **Review Video: Informative Text**
> Visit mometrix.com/academy and enter code: 924964

ENTERTAINMENT

The success or failure of an author's intent to entertain is determined by the reader. Entertaining texts may be either fiction or nonfiction, and may describe real or imagined people, places, and events. Entertaining texts are often narratives, or stories. A text that is written to entertain is likely to contain colorful language that engages the imagination and the emotions. Such writing often features a great deal of figurative language, enlivening its subject matter with images and analogies. Though an entertaining text is not usually written to persuade or inform, it may accomplish both of these tasks. An entertaining text may appeal to the reader's emotions and cause him or her to think differently about a particular subject. In any case, entertaining texts tend to showcase the personality of the author more than other types of writing.

EXPRESSION OF FEELINGS

When an author intends to express feelings, he/she may use colorful and evocative language. An author may write emotionally for any number of reasons. Sometimes, emotional language is used to describe a personal situation of great pain or happiness. Sometimes an author is attempting to persuade the reader, and so will use emotion to stir up the passions. It can be easy to identify this kind of expression when the writer uses phrases like *I felt* and *I sense*. However, sometimes the author will simply describe feelings without introducing them. As a reader, it is important to recognize when an author is expressing emotion, and not to be overwhelmed by sympathy or passion. A reader should maintain some detachment so that he or she can still evaluate the strength of the author's argument or the quality of the writing.

DESCRIPTION

Most writing is descriptive in a sense because it describes events, ideas, or people to the reader. Some texts, however, are primarily concerned with description. A descriptive text focuses on a particular subject and attempts to depict it in a way that will be clear to the reader. Descriptive texts contain many adjectives and adverbs, words that give shades of meaning and create a more detailed mental picture for the reader. A descriptive text fails when it is unclear or vague to the reader. On the other hand, a descriptive text that compiles too much detail can be boring and overwhelming to the reader. A descriptive text will certainly be informative, and it may be persuasive and entertaining as well. Descriptive writing is challenging, but when it is done well, it can be enjoyable to read.

WRITING DEVICES
COMPARING AND CONTRASTING

Authors will use different stylistic and writing devices to make their meaning more clearly understood. One of those devices is comparison and contrast. When an author describes how two things are alike, he or she is comparing them. When the author describes the ways in which two things are different, he or she is contrasting them. The "compare and contrast" essay is one of the most common forms in nonfiction. It is often signaled with certain words: a comparison may be indicated with such words as *both*, *same*, *like*, *too*, and *as well*; while a contrast may be indicated by words like *but*, *however*, *on the other hand*, *instead*, and *yet*. Of course, comparisons and contrasts may be implicit without any such signaling language. Also, a single sentence may both compare and contrast. Consider the sentence *Brian and Sheila love ice cream, but Brian prefers vanilla and Sheila prefers strawberry*. In one sentence, the author has described both a similarity (love of ice cream) and a difference (favorite flavor).

CAUSE AND EFFECT

One of the most common text structures is cause and effect. A cause is an act or event that makes something happen, and an effect is what happens as a result. A cause-and-effect relationship is not always explicit, but there are some words that signal causality, such as *since*, *because*, and *as a result*. Consider the sentence *Because the sky was clear, Ron did not bring an umbrella*. The cause is the clear sky, and the effect is that Ron did not bring an umbrella. However, sometimes the cause-and-effect relationship will not be clearly noted. For instance, the sentence *He was late and missed the meeting* does not contain any signaling words, but it still contains a cause (he was late) and an effect (he missed the meeting). It is possible for a single cause to have multiple effects, or for a single effect to have multiple causes. Also, an effect can in turn be the cause of another effect in what is known as a cause-and-effect chain.

ANALOGY

Authors often use analogies to add meaning to the text. An analogy is a comparison of two things. The words in the analogy are connected by a certain, often undetermined relationship. Look at this analogy: moo is to cow as quack is to duck. This analogy compares the sound that a cow makes with the sound that a duck makes. Even if the word 'quack' was not given, one could deduce that it is the correct word to complete the analogy based on the relationship between the words 'moo' and 'cow.' Some common relationships for analogies include synonyms, antonyms, part to whole, definition, and actor to action.

POINT OF VIEW

Another element that impacts a text is the author's point of view. A text's point of view is the perspective from which it is told. An author always has a point of view even before drawing up a plot line. The author will know what events will take place, how he/she wants the characters to interact, and how the story will resolve. An author will also have an opinion on the topic, or series of events, that is presented in the story, based on his/her own prior experience and beliefs.

The two main points of view that authors use are first person and third person. If the narrator of the story is also the main character, or *protagonist*, the text is written in first person. In first person, the author writes with the word *I*. A third-person point of view is probably the most common. Using third person, authors refer to each character using the words *he* or *she*. In third-person omniscient, the narrator is not a character in the story and tells the story of all of the characters with the same insight.

TRANSITIONAL WORDS

A good writer uses transitional words and phrases to guide the reader through the text. You are no doubt familiar with the common transitions, though you may never have considered how they operate. Some transitional phrases (*after*, *before*, *during*, *in the middle of*) give information about time. Some indicate that an example is about to be given (*for example*, *in fact*, *for instance*). Writers use them to compare (*also*, *likewise*) and contrast (*however*, *but*, *yet*). Transitional words and phrases can suggest addition (*and*, *also*, *furthermore*, *moreover*) and logical relationships (*if*, *then*, *therefore*, *as a result*, *since*). Finally, transitional words and phrases can demarcate the steps in a process (*first*, *second*, *last*). You should incorporate transitional words and phrases to orient your reader and explain the structure of your composition.

TYPES OF PASSAGES

NARRATIVE

A narrative passage is a story, fiction or nonfiction. To be classified as a narrative, a text must have a few key elements. To begin with, it must have a plot. That is, it must describe a series of events. If it is a good narrative, these events will be interesting and emotionally engaging to the reader. A narrative also has characters. These could be people, animals, or even inanimate objects, so long as they participate in the plot. A narrative passage often contains figurative language, which is meant to stimulate the imagination of the reader by making comparisons and observations. A metaphor, which uses one thing to describe another, is a common piece of figurative language. *The moon was a frosty snowball* is an example of a metaphor: it is obviously untrue in the literal sense, but it paints a vivid image for the reader. Narratives often proceed in a clear sequence, but may not always do so.

EXPOSITORY

An expository passage aims to inform and enlighten the reader. It is nonfiction and usually centers around a simple, easily defined topic. Since the goal of exposition is to teach, it should be as clear as possible. It is common for an expository passage to contain helpful organizing words like *first*, *next*, *for example*, and *therefore*. These words keep the reader oriented in the text. Although expository passages do not need to feature creative, descriptive writing, they are often more effective when they do. For a reader, the challenge of expository passages is to maintain steady attention. Expository passages are not always on subjects in which a reader is naturally interested, and the writer is often more concerned with clarity and comprehensibility than with engaging the reader. For this reason, many expository passages seem dull. Taking notes is a good way to maintain focus when reading an expository passage.

Review Video: Expository Passages
Visit mometrix.com/academy and enter code: 256515

TECHNICAL

A technical passage describes a complex object or process. Technical writing is common in medical and technological fields, in which complicated mathematical, scientific, and engineering ideas need to be explained simply and clearly. To aid comprehension, a technical passage usually follows a very logical order. Technical passages typically have clear headings and subheadings, helping to keep the reader oriented in the text. It is also common to organize sections by numbers or letters. Many technical passages look more like an outline than a piece of prose. The amount of jargon or difficult vocabulary in a technical passage varies, depending on the intended audience. As much as possible, technical passages try to avoid language that the reader will have to research to understand the message. Of course, it is not always possible to avoid jargon.

Review Video: A Technical Passage
Visit mometrix.com/academy and enter code: 478923

PERSUASIVE

A persuasive passage is meant to change the reader's mind or lead him/her into agreement with the author. The persuasive intent may be obvious, or it may be difficult to discern. In some cases, a persuasive passage will be indistinguishable from an informative passage: it will make an assertion and offer supporting details. However, a persuasive passage is more likely to make claims based on opinion and to appeal to the reader's emotions. Persuasive passages may not describe alternate positions or may display significant bias when they do. It may be clear that a persuasive passage is giving the author's viewpoint, or the passage may adopt a seemingly objective tone. A persuasive passage is successful if it can make a convincing argument and win the trust of the reader.

A persuasive essay will likely focus on one central argument, but it may make several smaller claims along the way. These are subordinate arguments with which the reader must agree if he or she is going to accept the central argument. The central argument is only as strong as the subordinate claims. These claims should be rooted in fact and observation, rather than subjective judgment. The best persuasive essays provide enough supporting detail to justify claims without overwhelming the reader. Remember that a fact must be susceptible to independent verification—it must be something the reader can confirm. Also, statistics are only effective when they take into account possible objections. For instance, a statistic on the number of foreclosed houses would only be useful if it was measured over a defined interval and in a defined area. Most readers are wary of statistics, because they are so often misleading. If possible, a persuasive essay should include references so that the reader can obtain more information. Of course, this means that the writer's accuracy and fairness may be judged by the inquiring reader, but giving references adds credence.

Opinions are formed by emotion as well as reason, and persuasive writers often appeal to the feelings of the reader. Although readers should always be skeptical of this technique, it is often used in a proper and ethical manner. For instance, many subjects have an obvious emotional component, and therefore cannot be fully covered without an appeal to the emotions. Consider an article on drunk driving: it makes sense to include specific examples that will alarm or sadden the reader. After all, drunk driving often has serious and tragic consequences. Emotional appeals are not appropriate, however, when they attempt to mislead the reader. For instance, in political advertisements it is common to emphasize the patriotism of the preferred candidate, because this will encourage the audience to link his/her own positive feelings about the country with his/her opinion of the candidate. However, these ads often falsely imply that the other candidate is unpatriotic. Another common and improper emotional appeal is the use of loaded language, such as referring to an avidly religious person as a "fanatic" or a passionate environmentalist as a "tree hugger." These terms introduce an emotional component that detracts from the argument.

RESPONDING TO LITERATURE
PREDICTION

When reading good literature, the reader is moved to engage actively in the text. One part of being an active reader involves making predictions. A prediction is a guess about what will happen next. Readers are constantly making predictions based on what they have read and what they already know. Consider the following sentence: *Staring at the computer screen in shock, Kim blindly reached for the brimming glass of water on the shelf beside her.* The sentence suggests that Kim is agitated and that she is not looking at the glass she is going to pick up, so a reader might predict that she is going to knock the glass over. Of course, not every prediction will be accurate: perhaps Kim will pick the glass up without incident. Nevertheless, the author has certainly created the expectation that the water might be spilled. Predictions are always subject to revision as the reader acquires more information.

> **Review Video: Predictions**
> Visit mometrix.com/academy and enter code: 437248

Test-taking tip: To respond to questions requiring future predictions, the student's answers should be based on evidence of past or present behavior.

INFERENCE

Readers are often required to understand text that claims and suggests ideas without stating them directly. An inference is a piece of information that is implied but not written outright by the author. For instance, consider the following sentence: *Mark made more money that week than he had in the previous year.* From this sentence, the reader can infer that Mark either did not make much money in the previous year or made a great deal of money that week. Often, a reader can use information he or she already knows to make inferences. Take as an example the sentence *When his coffee arrived, he looked around the table for the silver cup.* Many people know that cream is typically served in a silver cup, so using their own base of knowledge they can infer that the subject of this sentence takes his coffee with cream. Making inferences requires concentration, attention, and practice.

Test-taking tip: While being tested on his/her ability to make correct inferences, the student must look for contextual clues. An answer can be *true* but not *correct*. The contextual clues will help you choose the best answer out of the given choices. Understand the context in which a phrase is stated. When asked for the implied meaning of a statement made in the passage, the student should immediately locate the statement and read the context in which it was made. Also, look for an answer choice with a similar phrase to the statement in question.

SEQUENCE

A reader must be able to identify a text's sequence, or the order in which things happen. Often, and especially when the sequence is very important to the author, it is indicated with signal words like *first*, *then*, *next*, and *last*. However, sometimes a sequence is merely implied and must be noted by the reader. Consider the sentence *He walked in the front door and switched on the hall lamp.* Clearly, the man did not turn the lamp on before he walked in the door, so the implied sequence is that he first walked in the door and then turned on the lamp. Texts do not always proceed in an orderly sequence from first to last. Sometimes they begin at the end as a foreshadowing device and then start over at the beginning. As a reader, it can be useful to make brief notes to clarify the sequence.

Review Video: Sequence
Visit mometrix.com/academy and enter code: 489027

Review Video: Sequence of Events in a Story
Visit mometrix.com/academy and enter code: 807512

DRAWING CONCLUSIONS

In addition to inferring and predicting things about the text, the reader must often draw conclusions about the information he has read. When asked for a *conclusion*, look for critical "hedge" phrases such as *likely*, *may*, *can*, and *will often*, among others. When you are being tested on this knowledge, remember that question writers insert these hedge phrases to cover every possibility. Often an answer will be wrong simply because it leaves no room for exception. Extreme positive or negative answers (such as always, never, etc.) are usually not correct. The reader should not use any outside knowledge that is not gathered from the reading passage to answer the related questions. Correct answers can be drawn directly from the reading passage.

OPINIONS, FACTS, AND FALLACIES

Critical thinking skills are mastered through understanding various types of writing and the different purposes of authors. Every author writes for a purpose. Understanding that purpose, and how the author accomplishes a goal, will allow you to critique the writing and determine whether or not you agree with the conclusions.

FACT AND OPINION

Readers must always be conscious of the distinction between fact and opinion. A fact can be subjected to analysis and either proved or disproved. An opinion, on the other hand, is the author's personal feeling, which may not be proven by research, evidence, or argument. If the author writes that the distance from New York to Boston is about two hundred miles, he is stating a fact. But if he writes that New York is too crowded, then he is giving an opinion, because there is no objective standard for overpopulation. An opinion may be indicated by words like *believe*, *think*, or *feel*. Also, an opinion may be supported by facts. For instance, the author might give the population density of New York as a reason for why it is overcrowded. An opinion supported by fact tends to be more convincing. When authors support their opinions with other opinions, the reader is unlikely to be persuaded.

The author should present facts from reliable sources. An opinion is what the author thinks about a given topic. An opinion is not common knowledge or proven by expert sources, but it is information that the author believes and wants the reader to consider. To distinguish between fact and opinion, a reader needs to examine the type of source, what information backs up a claim, and whether or not the author may be motivated to convey a certain point of view. For example, if a panel of scientists has conducted multiple studies on the effectiveness of taking a certain vitamin, the results are more likely to be factual than if a company selling the vitamin claims that it can produce positive effects. The company is motivated to sell its product, while the scientists are examining it more objectively. If the author uses phrases such as "I think," the statement is an opinion.

In their attempt to persuade, writers often make mistakes in their thinking patterns and writing choices. It's important to understand these so you can make an informed decision. Every author has a point of view, but when he/she ignores reasonable counterarguments or distorts opposing viewpoints, this is demonstrating a bias. A bias is evident when the author is unfair or inaccurate in his or her presentation. Bias may be intentional or unintentional, but it should always alert the reader to question the argument. It should be noted that a biased author may still be correct. However, the author will be correct in spite of her bias, not because of it. A stereotype is like a bias, except that it is specifically applied to a group or place. Stereotyping is considered to be particularly abhorrent because it promotes negative generalizations about people. Many people are familiar with the negative stereotypes of certain ethnic, religious, and cultural groups. Readers should be very wary of authors who stereotype. These faulty assumptions typically reveal the author's ignorance and lack of curiosity or objectivity.

Sometimes, authors will appeal to the reader's emotion in an attempt to persuade or distract the reader from the argument's weakness. For instance, the author may try to inspire the reader's pity by delivering a heart-rending story. An author also might use the bandwagon approach, suggesting that his/her opinion is correct because it is held by the majority. Some authors resort to name-calling, in which insults and harsh words are delivered to the opponent in an attempt to distract. In advertising, a common appeal is the testimonial, in which a famous person endorses a product. Of course, the fact that a celebrity likes something should not really matter to the reader. These and other emotional appeals are usually evidence of poor reasoning and a weak argument.

LOGICAL FALLACIES

Certain *logical fallacies* are frequent in writing. A logical fallacy is a failure of reasoning. As a reader, it is important to recognize logical fallacies, because they diminish the value of the author's message. The four most common logical fallacies in writing are the false analogy, circular reasoning, false dichotomy, and overgeneralization. In a false analogy, the author suggests that two things are similar, when in fact they are different. This fallacy is often committed when the author is attempting to convince the reader that something unknown is like something relatively familiar. The author takes advantage of the reader's ignorance to make this false comparison. One example might be the following statement: *Failing to tip a waitress is like stealing money out of somebody's wallet.* Of course, failing to tip is very rude, especially when the service has been good, but people are not arrested for failing to tip as they would be for stealing money from a wallet. To compare stingy diners with thieves is a false analogy.

Circular reasoning is one of the more difficult logical fallacies to identify, because it is typically hidden behind dense language and complicated sentences. Reasoning is described as circular when it offers no support for assertions other than restating them in different words. Put another way, a circular argument uses itself as evidence of truth. A simple example of circular argument is when a person uses a word to define itself, such as saying *Niceness is the state of being nice*. If the reader does not know what *nice* means, then this definition will not be very useful. In a text, circular reasoning is usually more complex. For instance, an author might say, *Poverty is a problem for society because it creates trouble for people throughout the community*. It is redundant to say that poverty is a problem because it creates trouble. When an author engages in circular reasoning, it is often because he or she has not fully thought through the argument, or cannot come up with any legitimate justifications.

One of the most common logical fallacies is the false dichotomy, in which the author creates an artificial sense that there are only two possible alternatives in a situation. This fallacy is common when the author has an agenda and wants to give the impression that his/her view is the only sensible one. A false dichotomy has the effect of limiting the reader's options and imagination. An example is the statement *You need to go to the party with me, or you'll just be bored at home*. The speaker suggests that the only other possibility besides being at the party is being bored at home. This is not true, as it is possible to be entertained at home or to go somewhere other than the party. Readers should always be wary of the false dichotomy—when an author limits the alternatives, it is always wise to ask whether his argument valid.

Overgeneralization is a logical fallacy in which the author makes a claim so broad that it cannot be proved or disproved. In most cases, overgeneralization occurs when the author wants to create an illusion of authority, or when he/she is using sensational language to sway the reader's opinion. For instance, in the sentence *Everybody knows that she is a terrible teacher*, the author makes an assumption that cannot really be believed. The author is attempting to create the illusion of consensus when none actually exists. It may be that most people have a negative view of the teacher, but to say that *everybody* feels that way is an exaggeration. When a reader spots overgeneralization, she should become skeptical about the argument, because an author will often try to hide a weak or unsupported assertion behind authoritative language.

Two other types of logical fallacies are slippery slope arguments and hasty generalizations. In a slippery slope argument, the author says that if something happens, a certain result is guaranteed, even though this may not be true. For example, studying hard does not mean you are going to ace a test. Hasty generalization means drawing a conclusion too early, without finishing analysis of the argument's details. Writers of persuasive texts often use these techniques because they are very effective. In order to identify logical fallacies, readers need to read carefully and ask questions as they read. Thinking critically means not taking everything at face value. Readers need to critically evaluate an author's argument to make sure that the logic is sound.

ORGANIZATION OF TEXT

The way a text is organized can help the reader understand more clearly the author's intent and conclusions. There are various ways to organize a text, and each has its own purposes and uses.

PRESENTING A PROBLEM

Some nonfiction texts are organized to present a problem followed by a solution. In this type of text, it is common for the problem to be explained before the solution is offered. In some cases, as when the problem is well known, the solution may be briefly introduced at the beginning. The entire passage may focus on the solution, and the problem will be referenced only occasionally. Some texts

89

outline multiple solutions to a problem, leaving the reader to choose among them. If the author has an interest in or allegiance to one solution, he may fail to mention or may inaccurately describe other solutions. Readers should be careful of the author's agenda when reading a problem-solution text. Only by understanding the author's point of view and interests can one properly judge the proposed solution.

CHRONOLOGICAL ORDER

An author needs to organize information logically so the reader can follow it and locate information within the text. Two common organizational structures are cause and effect and chronological order. When using chronological order, the author presents information in the order that it happened. For example, biographies are written in chronological order; the subject's birth and childhood are presented first, followed by adult life, and finally the events leading up to death.

CAUSE AND EFFECT

In cause and effect, an author presents an event that causes something else to happen. For example, if one were to go to bed very late, he/she would be tired the next day. The cause is going to bed late, with the effect of being tired the next day.

It can be tricky to identify the cause-and-effect relationships in a text, but there are a few ways to approach this task. These relationships are often signaled with certain terms. When an author uses words like *because*, *since*, *in order*, and *so*, she is likely describing a cause-and-effect relationship. Consider the sentence, "He called her because he needed the homework." This is a simple causal relationship, in which the cause was his need for the homework and the effect was his phone call. Not all cause-and-effect relationships are marked in this way, however. Consider the sentences, "He called her. He needed the homework." When the cause-and-effect relationship is not indicated with a keyword, it can be discovered by asking why something happened. Why did he call? The answer is in the next sentence—he needed the homework.

Persuasive essays, in which an author tries to make a convincing argument and change the reader's mind, usually include cause-and-effect relationships. However, these relationships should not always be taken at face value. An author frequently assumes a cause or takes an effect for granted. To read a persuasive essay effectively, one needs to judge the cause-and-effect relationships the author is presenting. For instance, an author could write the following: "The parking deck has been unprofitable because people prefer to ride their bikes." The relationship is clear: the cause is that people prefer to ride their bikes, and the effect is that the parking deck has been unprofitable. However, a reader should consider whether this argument is conclusive. There could be other reasons for the failure of the parking deck: a down economy, excessive fees, etc. Too often, authors present causal relationships as if they are fact rather than opinion. Readers should be on the alert for these dubious claims.

COMPARISON AND CONTRAST

Thinking critically about ideas and conclusions can seem like a daunting task. One way to make it easier is to understand the basic elements of ideas and writing techniques. Looking at the way different ideas relate to each other is a good way for the reader to begin his/her analysis. For instance, an author may write about two opposing ideas. Analyzing these is known as contrast. Contrast is often marred by the author's obvious partiality to one of the ideas. A discerning reader will be put off by an author who does not "fight fairly." In an analysis of opposing ideas, both ideas should be presented in their clearest and most reasonable terms. If the author does prefer a side, he/she should avoid indicating this preference with pejorative language. An analysis of opposing ideas should proceed through the major differences point by point, with a full explanation of each side. For instance, in an analysis of capitalism and communism, it would be important to outline each side's view on labor, markets, prices, personal responsibility, etc. It would be less effective to describe the theory of communism and then explain how capitalism has thrived in the West. An analysis of opposing views should present each side in the same manner.

Many texts follow the compare-and-contrast model, exploring the similarities and differences between two ideas or things. Analysis of the similarities is called comparison. In order for a comparison to work, the author must place the ideas or things in an equivalent structure. That is, the author must present the ideas in the same way. Imagine an author wanted to show the similarities between cricket and baseball. He/she could do this by summarizing the equipment and rules for each game. It would be incorrect to summarize the equipment of cricket and then tell the history of baseball, since this would make it impossible for the reader to see the similarities. It is perhaps too obvious to say that an analysis of similar ideas should emphasize the similarities. Of course, the author should also include differences. Often, these small differences will only reinforce the more general similarity.

DRAWING CONCLUSIONS
IDENTIFYING THE LOGICAL CONCLUSION

An author should have a clear purpose in mind while writing. Especially when reading informational texts, it is important to understand the logical conclusion of the author's ideas. Identifying this logical conclusion can help the reader understand whether he/she agrees with the writer or not. It is much like making an inference: it requires the reader to combine the information given by the text with what he already knows to make a supportable assertion. If a passage is written well, the conclusion should be obvious even when it is unstated. If the author intends the reader to draw a certain conclusion, then all argumentation and detail should lead toward it. One way to approach the task of drawing conclusions is to make brief notes of all the author's points. When these are arranged on paper, they may clarify the logical conclusion. Another way to approach conclusions is to consider whether the author's reasoning raises any pertinent questions. Sometimes it is possible to draw multiple conclusions from a passage, and on occasion these were never intended by the author. It is essential, however, that these conclusions be supported directly by the text.

> **Review Video: Identifying Logical Conclusions**
> Visit mometrix.com/academy and enter code: 281653

TEXT EVIDENCE

The term *text evidence* refers to information that supports a main point or points in a story and can guide the reader to a conclusion. Information used as text evidence is precise, descriptive, and factual. A main point is often followed by supporting details that provide evidence to back up a claim. For example, a story may include the claim that winter occurs during opposite months in the Northern and Southern hemispheres. Text evidence based on this claim may include countries where winter occurs in opposite months, along with the reasons (the tilt of the earth as it rotates around the sun).

> **Review Video: Text Evidence**
> Visit mometrix.com/academy and enter code: 486236

Readers interpret text and respond in a number of ways. Using textual support helps defend your response or interpretation because it roots your thinking in the text. You are interpreting based on information in the text and not simply your own ideas. When crafting a response, look for important quotes and details from the text to bolster your argument. If you are writing about a character's personality trait, for example, use details from the text to show how the character displayed this trait. You can also include statistics and facts from a nonfiction text to strengthen your response. For example, instead of writing, "A lot of people use cell phones," use statistics to provide a specific number. This strengthens your argument because it is more precise.

CREDIBILITY

The text used to support an argument can be the argument's downfall if it is not credible. A text is credible, or believable, when the author is knowledgeable and objective, or unbiased. The author's motivations for writing play a critical role in determining the credibility of the text and must be evaluated when assessing that credibility. The author's motives should be simply to disseminate information. The purpose of the text should be to inform or describe, not to persuade. When an author writes a persuasive text, his/her motivation is to convince the reader to do what he/she wants. The extent of the author's knowledge and motivation must be evaluated when assessing the credibility of a text. Reports written about the ozone layer by an environmental scientist and a hairdresser will have a different level of credibility.

> **Review Video: Credible**
> Visit mometrix.com/academy and enter code: 827257

RESPONSE TO TEXT

After determining your own opinion and evaluating the credibility of your supporting text, it is sometimes necessary to communicate your ideas and findings to others. When writing a response to a text, it is important to use elements of the text to support your assertion or defend your position. Using supporting evidence from the text strengthens the argument because it shows that you read the original piece in depth and based your response on the details and facts within that text. Elements of text that can be used in a response include: facts, details, statistics, and direct quotations. When writing a response, one must indicate which information comes from the original text and then base the discussion, argument, or defense around this information.

DIRECTLY STATED INFORMATION

A reader should constantly draw conclusions from the text. Sometimes conclusions are implied from written information, and other times the information is stated directly within the passage. It is always stronger to draw conclusions from information stated within a passage, rather than from mere implications. At times an author may provide some information and then describe a counterargument. The reader should be alert for direct statements that are subsequently rejected or weakened by the author and should always read the entire passage before drawing conclusions. Many readers are trained to expect the author's conclusions at either the beginning or the end of the passage, but many texts do not adhere to this format.

IMPLICATIONS

Drawing conclusions from information implied within a passage requires the reader's confidence. Implications are things the author does not state directly, but that can be assumed based on what the author does say. For instance, consider the following simple passage: "I stepped outside and opened my umbrella. By the time I got to work, the cuffs of my pants were soaked." The author never states that it is raining, but this fact is clearly implied. Conclusions based on implication must be well supported by the text. In order to draw a solid conclusion, a reader should have multiple pieces of evidence, or, if he only has one, must be assured that there is no other possible explanation than his conclusion. A good reader will be able to draw many conclusions from information implied by the text, which enriches the reading experience considerably.

OUTLINING

As an aid to drawing conclusions, the reader should be adept at outlining the information contained in the passage; an effective outline will reveal the structure of the passage, and will lead to solid conclusions. An effective outline will have a title referencing the basic subject of the text, though it need not repeat the main idea. In most outlines, the main idea is the first major section. It will establish each major idea of the passage as the head of a category. The most common outline format indicates the main ideas of the passage with Roman numerals. None of the Roman numerals will designate minor details or secondary ideas. Moreover, all supporting ideas and details should be placed in the appropriate section on the outline. An outline does not need to include every detail listed in the text, but it should feature all that are central to the argument or message. Each details should be listed under the appropriate main idea.

> **Review Video: Outlining**
> Visit mometrix.com/academy and enter code: 584445

SUMMARY

It is also helpful to summarize the information in paragraph or passage format. This process is similar to creating an effective outline. To begin with, a summary should accurately define the main idea of the passage, though it does not need to explain it in exhaustive detail. It should continue by laying out the most important supporting details or arguments from the passage. All significant supporting details should be included, but no irrelevant or insignificant details. Also, the summary must accurately report these details. Too often, the desire for brevity in a summary leads to the sacrifice of clarity or veracity. Summaries are often difficult to read, because they omit all the graceful language, descriptions, and asides that distinguish great writing. However, if the summary is effective, it should contain the same message as the original text.

> **Review Video: Summarizing Text**
> Visit mometrix.com/academy and enter code: 172903

PARAPHRASING

Paraphrasing is another method the reader can use to aid comprehension. When paraphrasing, one rephrases what the author has written in his/her own words, "translating" the author's message and including as many details as possible.

INFORMATIONAL SOURCES

Informational sources may come in short forms like memos and articles or longer forms like books, magazines, and journals. These longer sources of information each have their own way of organizing information, but there are some similarities that the reader should be aware of.

TABLE OF CONTENTS

Most books, magazines, and journals have a table of contents at the beginning. This helps the reader find the different parts of the book. The table of contents is usually found a page or two after the title page in a book, and on the first few pages of a magazine. However, many magazines now place the table of contents in the midst of advertisements, because they know readers will have to look at the ads as they search for the table. The standard orientation for a table of contents has the sections of the book listed along the left side, with the initial page number for each along the right. It is common in a book for the prefatory material (preface, introduction, etc.) to be numbered with Roman numerals. The contents are always listed in order from the beginning of the book to the end.

INDEX

A nonfiction book also typically has an index at the end so that the reader can easily find information on particular topics. An index lists the topics in alphabetical order. The names of people are listed with the last name first. For example, *Adams, John* would come before *Washington, George*. To the right of the entry, the relevant page numbers are listed. When a topic is mentioned over several pages, the index will often connect these pages with a dash. For instance, if the subject is mentioned from pages 35 to 42 and again on 53, then the index entry will be labeled as *35–42, 53*. Some entries will have subsets, which are listed below the main entry, indented slightly, and placed in alphabetical order. This is common for subjects that are discussed frequently in the book. For instance, in a book about Elizabethan drama, William Shakespeare will likely be an important topic. Beneath Shakespeare's name in the index, there might be listings for *death of, dramatic works of, life of*, etc. These more specific entries help the reader refine his search.

HEADINGS AND SUBHEADINGS

Many informative texts, especially textbooks, use headings and subheadings for organization. Headings and subheadings are typically printed in larger and bolder fonts (or all capitals), and are often in a different color than the main body of the text. Headings may be larger than subheadings. Also, headings and subheadings are not always complete sentences. A heading announces the topic that will be addressed in the text below. Headings are meant to alert the reader to what is about to come. Subheadings announce the topics of smaller sections within the entire section indicated by the heading. For instance, the heading of a section in a science textbook might be *AMPHIBIANS*, and within that section might be subheadings for *Frogs, Salamanders*, and *Newts*. Readers should always pay close attention to headings and subheadings, because they prime the brain for the information that is about to be delivered, and because they make it easy to go back and find particular details in a long text.

REFERENCE MATERIALS

DICTIONARIES

Knowledge of reference materials such as dictionaries, encyclopedias, and manuals is vital for any reader. Dictionaries contain a multitude of information about words. A standard dictionary entry begins with a pronunciation guide for the word. The entry will also give the word's part of speech (noun, verb, adjective, etc.). A good dictionary will also include the word's etymology, or origin, including the language from which it is derived and its meaning in that language.

Dictionary entries are in alphabetical order. Many words have more than one definition, in which case the definitions will be numbered. Also, if a word can be used as different parts of speech, its various definitions may be separated. A sample entry might look like this:

> WELL: (adverb) 1. in a good way (noun) 1. a hole drilled into the earth

The correct definition of a word will vary depending on how it is used in a sentence. When looking up a word found while reading, the best way to determine the relevant definition is to substitute the dictionary's definitions for the word in the text, and select the definition that seems most appropriate.

ENCYCLOPEDIAS

Encyclopedias used to be the best source for general information on a range of common subjects. Many people took pride in owning a set of encyclopedias, which were often written by top researchers. Now, encyclopedias largely exist online. Although they no longer have a preeminent place in general scholarship, these digital encyclopedias now often feature audio and video clips. A good encyclopedia remains the best place to obtain basic information about a well-known topic. There are also specialty encyclopedias that cover more obscure or expert information. For instance, medical encyclopedias contain the detail and sophistication required by doctors. For a regular person researching a subject like ostriches, Pennsylvania, or the Crimean War, a basic encyclopedia is a good source.

THESAURUS

A thesaurus is a reference book that gives synonyms of words. Unlike a dictionary, a thesaurus does not give definitions, only lists of synonyms. A thesaurus can be helpful in finding the meaning of an unfamiliar word when reading. If the meaning of a synonym is known, then the meaning of the unfamiliar word can be inferred. A thesaurus is also helpful when writing. Using a thesaurus helps authors to vary their word choice.

DATABASE

A database is an informational source with a different format than a publication or a memo. It is a system for storing and organizing large amounts of information. As personal computers have become more common and accessible, databases have become ever more present. The standard layout of a database is a grid, with labels along the left side and top. The horizontal rows and vertical columns that make up the grid are usually numbered or lettered, so that a particular square within the database might be referenced as A3 or G5. Databases are good for storing information that can be expressed succinctly. They are most commonly used to store numerical data but can also be used to store the answers to yes/no questions and other brief data points. Information that is ambiguous (multiple possible meanings) or difficult to express in a few words is not appropriate for a database.

CONTEXT

Often, a reader will come across a word he/she does not recognize. It is important to be able to identify a word's definition from its context. This means defining a word based on the words around it and the way it is used in a sentence. Consider the following sentence: *The elderly scholar spent his evenings hunched over arcane texts that few other people even knew existed.* The adjective *arcane* is uncommon, but the reader can obtain significant information about it based on its use here. Because few other people know of the texts' existence, the reader can assume that arcane texts must be rare and only of interest to a few people. Because they are being read by an elderly scholar, the reader can assume that they focus on difficult academic subjects. Sometimes, words can even be defined by process of elimination. Consider the following sentence: *Ron's fealty to his parents was not shared by Karen, who disobeyed their every command.* Because someone who disobeys is not demonstrating *fealty*, the word can be inferred to mean obedience or respect.

PRIMARY SOURCES

When conducting research, it is important to use reputable primary sources. A primary source is the documentary evidence closest to the subject being studied. For instance, the primary sources for an essay about penguins would be photographs and recordings of the birds, as well as accounts of people who have studied penguins in person. A secondary source would be a review of a movie about penguins or a book outlining the observations made by others. A primary source should be credible and, if it is on a subject that is still being explored, recent. One way to assess the credibility of a work is to see how often it is mentioned in other books and articles on the same subject. By reading the works cited and bibliography sections of other books, one can get a sense of the acknowledged authorities in the field.

INTERNET

The Internet was once considered an unreliable place to find sources for an essay or article, but its credibility has improved greatly over the years. Still, students need to exercise caution when researching online. The best sources are those affiliated with established institutions, like universities, public libraries, and think tanks. Most newspapers are available online, and many of them allow the public to browse their archives. Magazines frequently offer similar services. When obtaining information from an unknown website, however, one must exercise considerably more caution. A website can be considered trustworthy if it is referenced by other reputable sites. Also, credible sites tend to be properly maintained and frequently updated. A site is easier to trust when the author provides some information about him or herself, including some credentials that indicate expertise in the subject matter.

ORGANIZING AND UNDERSTANDING GRAPHIC INFORMATION

Two of the most common ways to organize ideas from a text, paraphrasing and summarizing, are verbal organizational methods. Graphic organizers are also useful in arranging ideas from a text. A graphic organizer is a way to simplify information and take only key points from the text. A graphic organizer such as a timeline may have an event listed for a corresponding date on the timeline, whereas an outline may have an event listed under a key point that occurs in the text. Each reader needs to create the type of graphic organizer that works the best for him or her—the method that will best aid in recalling information from a story. Examples include a *spider-map*, which takes a main idea from the story and places it in a bubble, with supporting points branching off the main idea, an *outline,* useful for diagramming the main and supporting points of the entire story, and a *Venn diagram*, which classifies information as separate or overlapping.

> **Review Video: Graphic Organizers**
> Visit mometrix.com/academy and enter code: 665513

Authors can also use these graphic organizers to enliven their presentation or text, but this may be counterproductive if the graphics are confusing or misleading. A graph should strip the author's message down to the essentials. It should have a clear title and should be in the appropriate format. Authors may elect to use tables, line or bar graphs, or pie charts to illustrate their message. Each of these formats is correct for different types of data. The graphic should be large enough to read and should be divided into appropriate categories. For instance, if the text discusses the differences between federal spending on the military and on the space program, a pie chart or a bar graph would be the most effective choices. The pie chart could show each type of spending as a portion of total federal spending, while the bar graph would be better for directly comparing the amounts of money spent on these two programs.

In most cases, the work of interpreting information presented in graphs, tables, charts, and diagrams is done for the reader. The author usually makes clear his or her reasons for presenting a certain set of data in such a way. However, an effective reader will avoid taking the author's claims for granted. Before considering the information presented in the graphic, the reader should consider whether the author has chosen the correct format for presentation, or whether the author has omitted variables or other information that might undermine his case. Interpreting the graphic itself is essentially an exercise in spotting trends. On a graph, for instance, the reader should be alert for how one variable responds to a change in the other. If education level increases, for example, does income increase as well? The same can be done for a table. Readers should be alert for values that break or exaggerate a trend; these may be meaningless outliers or indicators of a change in conditions.

When a reader is required to draw conclusions from the information presented in graphs, tables, charts, or diagrams, it is important to limit these conclusions to the terms of the graphic itself. In other words, the reader should avoid extrapolating from the data to make claims that are not supportable. As an example, consider a graph that compares the price of eggs to the demand. If the price and demand rise and fall together, a reader would be justified in saying that the demand for eggs and the price are tied together. However, this simple graph does not indicate which of these variables causes the other, so the reader would not be justified in concluding that the price of eggs raises or lowers the demand, as demand could be tied to a multitude of other factors not included in the chart.

TABLES AND CHARTS
TABLES

Tables are presented in a standard format so they will be easy to read and understand. A title is at the top, a short phrase indicating the information the table or graph intends to convey. The title of a table could be something like "Average Income for Various Education Levels" or "Price of Milk Compared to Demand." A table is composed of information laid out in vertical columns and horizontal rows. Typically, each column will have a label. If "Average Income for Various Education Levels" was placed in a table format, the two columns could be labeled "Education Level" and "Average Income." Each location on the table is called a cell, which holds a piece of information. Cells are defined by their column and row (e.g., second column, fifth row).

GRAPHS

Like a table, a graph typically has a title at the top. This title may simply state the identities of the two axes: e.g., "Income vs. Education." However, the title may also be something more descriptive, like "A comparison of average income with level of education." In any case, bar and line graphs are laid out along two perpendicular lines, or axes. The vertical axis is called the y-axis, and the horizontal axis is called the x-axis. It is typical for the x-axis to be the independent variable and the y-axis to be the dependent variable. The independent variable is the one manipulated by the researcher or creator of the graph. In the above example, the independent variable would be "level of education," since the maker of the graph will define these values (high school, college, master's degree, etc.). The dependent value is not controlled by the researcher.

When selecting a graph format, it is important to consider the intention and the structure of the presentation. A bar graph is appropriate for displaying the relations between a series of distinct quantities that are on the same scale. For instance, if one wanted to display the amount of money spent on groceries during the months of a year, a bar graph would be appropriate. The vertical axis would represent values of money, and the horizontal axis would identify each month. A line graph also requires data expressed in common units, but it is better for demonstrating the general trend in that data. If the grocery expenses were plotted on a line graph instead of a bar graph, there would be more emphasis on whether the amount of money spent rose or fell over the course of the year. Whereas a bar graph is good for showing the relationships between the different values plotted, the line graph is good for showing whether the values tended to increase, decrease, or remain stable.

LINE GRAPH

A line graph is typically used for measuring trends over time. It is set up along a vertical and horizontal axis. The variables being measured are listed along the left and bottom sides of the axes. Points are then plotted along the graph to correspond with their values for each variable. For instance, imagine a line graph measuring a person's income for each month of the year. If the person earned $1500 in January, there would be a point directly above January and directly to the right of $1500. Once all of the lines are plotted, they are connected with a line from left to right. This

97

line provides a nice visual illustration of the general trends. For instance, if the line sloped up, it would indicate that the person's income had increased over the course of the year.

BAR GRAPH

The bar graph is one of the most common visual representations of information. Bar graphs are used to illustrate sets of numerical data. The graph has a vertical axis, along which numbers are listed, and a horizontal axis, along which categories, words, or some other indicators are placed. An example of a bar graph is a depiction of the respective heights of famous basketball players: the vertical axis would contain numbers ranging from five to eight feet, and the horizontal axis would contain the names of the players. The length of the bar above the player's name would illustrate his height, lining up with the number listed along the left side. In this representation, then, it would be easy to see that Yao Ming is taller than Michael Jordan, because Yao's bar would be higher.

PIE CHART

A pie chart, also known as a circle graph, is useful for depicting how a single unit or category is divided. The standard pie chart is a circle divided into wedges. Each of these wedges is proportional in size to its part of the whole. Consider a pie chart representing a student's budget. If the student spends half her money on rent, then the pie chart will represent that amount with a line through the center of the pie. If she spends a quarter of her money on food, there will be a line extending from the edge of the circle to the center at a right angle to the line depicting rent. This illustration would make it clear that the student spends twice as much money on rent as she does on food. The pie chart is only appropriate for showing how a whole is divided, not for demonstrating the relationships between parts of different wholes. For example, it would not be helpful to use a pie chart to compare the respective amounts of state and federal spending devoted to infrastructure, since these values are only meaningful in the context of the entire budget.

DETERMINING WORD MEANING

An understanding of the basics of language is helpful, and often vital, to understanding what you read. *Structural analysis* refers to looking at the parts of a word and breaking it down into its different components to determine the meaning. By learning the meanings of word fundamentals, you can decipher the meaning of words that may not yet be in your vocabulary. Parts of a word include prefixes, suffixes, and the root word. Prefixes are common letter combinations at the beginning of words, while suffixes are common letter combinations at the end. The main part of the word is known as the root. Visually, it would look like this: prefix + root word + suffix. Look first at the individual meanings of the root word, prefix and/or suffix. Use knowledge of the meaning(s) of the prefix and/or suffix to see what information it adds to the root. Even if the meaning of the root is unknown, one can use knowledge of the prefix and/or suffix to determine an approximate meaning of the word. For example, if one sees the word *uninspired* and does not know what it means, they can use the knowledge that *un-* means 'not' to know that the full word means "not inspired." Understanding the common prefixes and suffixes can illuminate at least part of the meaning of an unfamiliar word.

Below is a list of common prefixes and their meanings:

Prefix	Definition	Examples
a-	in, on, of, up, to	abed, afoot
a-	without, lacking	atheist, agnostic
ab-	from, away, off	abdicate, abjure
ad-	to, toward	advance

Prefix	Definition	Examples
am-	friend, love	amicable, amatory
ante-	before, previous	antecedent, antedate
anti-	against, opposing	antipathy, antidote
auto-	self	autonomy, autobiography
belli-	war, warlike	bellicose
bene-	well, good	benefit, benefactor
bi-	two	bisect, biennial
bio-	life	biology, biosphere
cata-	down, away, thoroughly	catastrophe, cataclysm
chron-	time	chronometer, chronology
circum-	around	circumspect, circumference
com-	with, together, very	commotion, complicate
contra-	against, opposing	contradict, contravene
cred-	belief, trust	credible, credit
de-	from	depart
dem-	people	demographics, democracy
dia-	through, across, apart	diameter, diagnose
dis-	away, off, down, not	dissent, disappear
epi-	upon	epilogue
equi-	equal, equally	equivalent
ex-	out	extract
for-	away, off, from	forget, forswear
fore-	before, previous	foretell, forefathers
homo-	same, equal	homogenized
hyper-	excessive, over	hypercritical, hypertension
hypo-	under, beneath	hypodermic, hypothesis
in-	in, into	intrude, invade
in-	not, opposing	incapable, ineligible
inter-	among, between	intercede, interrupt
intra-	within	intramural, intrastate
magn-	large	magnitude, magnify
mal-	bad, poorly, not	malfunction
micr-	small	microbe, microscope
mis-	bad, poorly, not	misspell, misfire
mono-	one, single	monogamy, monologue
mort-	die, death	mortality, mortuary
neo-	new	neolithic, neoconservative
non-	not	nonentity, nonsense
ob-	against, opposing	objection
omni-	all, everywhere	omniscient
ortho-	right, straight	orthogonal, orthodox
over-	above	overbearing
pan-	all, entire	panorama, pandemonium

Prefix	Definition	Examples
para-	beside, beyond	parallel, paradox
per-	through	perceive, permit
peri-	around	periscope, perimeter
phil-	love, like	philosophy, philanthropic
poly-	many	polymorphous, polygamous
post-	after, following	postpone, postscript
pre-	before, previous	prevent, preclude
prim-	first, early	primitive, primary
pro-	forward, in place of	propel, pronoun
re-	back, backward, again	revoke, recur
retro-	back, backward	retrospect, retrograde
semi-	half, partly	semicircle, semicolon
sub-	under, beneath	subjugate, substitute
super-	above, extra	supersede, supernumerary
sym-	with, together	sympathy, symphony
trans-	across, beyond, over	transact, transport
ultra-	beyond, excessively	ultramodern, ultrasonic, ultraviolet
un-	not, reverse of	unhappy, unlock
uni-	one	uniform, unity
vis-	to see	visage, visible

Below is a list of common suffixes and their meanings:

Suffix	Definition	Examples
-able	able to, likely	capable, tolerable
-age	process, state, rank	passage, bondage
-ance	act, condition, fact	acceptance, vigilance
-arch	to rule	monarch, oligarch
-ard	one that does excessively	drunkard, wizard
-ate	having, showing	separate, desolate
-ation	action, state, result	occupation, starvation
-cy	state, condition	accuracy, captaincy
-dom	state, rank, condition	serfdom, wisdom
-en	cause to be, become	deepen, strengthen
-er	one who does	teacher, lawyer
-esce	become, grow, continue	convalesce, acquiesce
-esque	in the style of, like	picturesque, grotesque
-ess	feminine	waitress, lioness
-fic	making, causing	terrific, beatific
-ful	full of, marked by	thankful, beautiful
-fy	make, cause, cause to have	glorify, fortify
-hood	state, condition	manhood, statehood
-ible	able, likely, fit	edible, possible, divisible
-ion	action, result, state	union, fusion

Suffix	Definition	Examples
-ish	suggesting, like	churlish, childish
-ism	act, manner, doctrine	barbarism, socialism
-ist	doer, believer	monopolist, socialist
-ition	action, state, result	sedition, expedition
-ity	state, quality, condition	acidity, civility
-ize	make, cause to be, treat with	sterilize, mechanize, criticize
-less	lacking, without	hopeless, countless
-like	like, similar	childlike, dreamlike
-logue	type of written/spoken language	prologue, monologue
-ly	like, of the nature of	friendly, positively
-ment	means, result, action	refreshment, disappointment
-ness	quality, state	greatness, tallness
-or	doer, office, action	juror, elevator, honor
-ous	marked by, given to	religious, riotous
-ship	the art or skill of	statesmanship
-some	apt to, showing	tiresome, lonesome
-th	act, state, quality	warmth, width
-tude	quality, state, result	magnitude, fortitude
-ty	quality, state	enmity, activity
-ward	in the direction of	backward, homeward

The more words a person is exposed to, the greater his/her vocabulary will become. By reading on a regular basis, a person can see words in context in a variety of different ways. Based on experience, a person can recall how a word was used in the past and apply that knowledge to a new context. For example, a person may have seen the word *gull* used to mean a bird that is found near the seashore. However, a *gull* can also be a person who is easily tricked. If the word is used in context in reference to a character, the reader can recognize that the character is being called a bird that is not seen as extremely intelligent. What a reader knows about a word can be useful when making comparisons or figuring out the meaning of a new use of a word, as in figurative language, idioms, analogies, and multiple-meaning words.

DENOTATIVE AND CONNOTATIVE MEANING

When defining words in a text, words often have a meaning that is more than the dictionary definition. The denotative meaning of a word is the literal meaning. The connotative meaning goes beyond the denotative meaning to include the emotional reaction a word may invoke, due to associations the reader makes with the denotative meaning. The reader can differentiate between the denotative and connotative meanings by first recognizing when authors use each meaning. Most nonfiction, for example, is fact-based, and the authors typically do not use flowery, figurative language. The reader can assume that the writer is using the denotative, or literal, meaning of words. In fiction, on the other hand, the author may be using the connotative meaning, as connotation is one form of figurative language. The reader should use context clues to determine whether the author is using the denotative or connotative meaning of a word.

CONTEXT

Readers of all levels encounter words with which they are somewhat unfamiliar. The best way to define a word in context is to look for nearby words for clues. For instance, unfamiliar nouns are often accompanied by examples that furnish a definition. Consider the following sentence: "Dave arrived at the party in hilarious garb: a leopard-print shirt, buckskin trousers, and high heels." If a reader was unfamiliar with the meaning of garb, he could read the examples and quickly determine that the word means "clothing." Examples will not always be this obvious. For instance, consider this sentence: "Parsley, lemon, and flowers were just a few of items he used as garnishes." Here, the possibly unfamiliar word *garnishes* is exemplified by parsley, lemon, and flowers. Readers who have eaten in a variety of restaurants can identify a garnish as something used to decorate a plate.

It is sometimes possible to define an unfamiliar word by looking at the descriptive words in context. Consider the following sentence: "Fred dragged the recalcitrant boy kicking and screaming up the stairs." *Dragged*, *kicking*, and *screaming* all suggest that the boy does not want to go up the stairs. The reader may assume that *recalcitrant* means something like unwilling or protesting. In that example, an unfamiliar adjective was identified. It is perhaps more typical to use description to define an unfamiliar noun, as in this sentence: "Don's wrinkled frown and constantly shaking fist identified him as a curmudgeon of the first order." Don is described as having a "wrinkled frown and constantly shaking fist," suggesting that a *curmudgeon* must be a grumpy old man. Context does not always provide detailed information about the unfamiliar word, but can at least give the reader some clues.

CONTRASTS

In addition to looking at the context of a passage, readers can often use contrasts to define an unfamiliar word in context. In many sentences, the author will not describe the unfamiliar word directly, but will instead describe the opposite of the unfamiliar word. Of course, this provides information about the word the reader needs to define. Consider the following example: "Despite his intelligence, Hector's low brow and bad posture made him look obtuse." The author suggests that Hector's appearance was opposite to his actual intelligence. Therefore, *obtuse* must mean unintelligent or stupid. Here is another example: "Despite the horrible weather, we were beatific about our trip to Alaska." The word *despite* indicates that the speaker's feelings were at odds with the weather. Since the weather is described as "horrible," *beatific* must mean something pleasant.

SUBSTITUTION

In some cases, there will be very few contextual clues to help a reader define an unfamiliar word. When this happens, one useful strategy is substitution. A good reader can brainstorm possible synonyms for the given word, and then substitute these words into the sentence. If the sentence and the surrounding passage continue to make sense, the substitution has revealed at least some information about the unfamiliar word. Consider the sentence, "Frank's admonition rang in her ears as she climbed the mountain." A reader unfamiliar with *admonition* might come up with some substitutions like "vow," "promise," "advice," "complaint," or "compliment." All of these words make general sense of the sentence, though their meanings are diverse. The process has suggested, however, that an admonition is some sort of message. The substitution strategy is rarely able to pinpoint a precise definition, but can be effective as a last resort.

MULTIPLE MEANING WORDS

When a word has more than one meaning, it can be tricky to determine its meaning in a given sentence. Consider the verb *cleave*, which can mean either "join" or "separate." When a reader comes upon this word, he/she must select the definition that makes the most sense. So, take as an example the following sentence: "The birds cleaved together as they flew from the oak tree." Immediately, the presence of the word *together* should suggest that in this sentence *cleave* is being used to mean "*join*." A slightly more difficult example is "Hermione's knife cleaved the bread cleanly." It doesn't make sense for a knife to join bread together, so the word must be meant to indicate separation. Discovering the meaning of a word with multiple meanings requires the same tricks as defining an unknown word: looking for contextual clues and evaluating substituted words.

LITERARY DEVICES

SYNONYMS AND ANTONYMS

Understanding how words relate to each other can often add meaning to a passage. This is explained by understanding synonyms (words that mean the same thing) and antonyms (words that mean the opposite). As an example, *dry* and *arid* are synonyms, and *dry* and *wet* are antonyms. There are many pairs of words that can be considered synonyms, despite having slightly different definitions. For instance, the words *friendly* and *collegial* can both be used to describe a warm interpersonal relationship, so it would be correct to call them synonyms. However, *collegial* (kin to *colleague*) is more often used in reference to professional or academic relationships, while *friendly* has no such connotation. Nevertheless, it would be appropriate to call these words synonyms. If the difference between the two words is too great, however, they may not be called synonyms. *Hot* and *warm* are not synonyms, for instance, because their meanings are too distinct. A good way to determine whether two words are synonyms is to substitute one for the other and see if the sentence means the same thing. Substituting *warm* for *hot* in a sentence would convey a different meaning.

Antonyms are opposites. *Light* and *dark*, *up* and *down*, *right* and *left*, *good* and *bad*: these are all sets of antonyms. It is important to distinguish between antonyms and pairs of words that are simply different. *Black* and *gray*, for instance, are not antonyms because gray is not the opposite of black. *Black* and *white*, on the other hand, are antonyms. Not every word has an antonym. Nouns in particular do not often have antonyms, as there is no "opposite" for humans, places, objects, etc. On a standardized test, the questions related to antonyms are more likely to concern adjectives, which describe nouns. Some common adjectives include *red*, *fast*, *skinny*, and *sweet*. Of these four examples, only *red* lacks a group of obvious antonyms.

> **Review Video: Synonyms and Antonyms**
> Visit mometrix.com/academy and enter code: 105612

FIGURATIVE LANGUAGE

Authors use many types of language devices to convey their meaning in a more descriptive or interesting way. Understanding these concepts will help you understand what you read. These devices are called *figurative language*—language that goes beyond the literal meaning of the words. Descriptive language that evokes imagery in the reader's mind is one type of figurative language. Exaggeration and comparison are other types. Similes and metaphors are types of comparison, commonly found in poetry. An example of figurative language (a simile in this case) is: "The child howled like a coyote when her mother told her to pick up the toys." In this example, the child's howling is compared to that of a coyote. Figurative language is descriptive in nature and helps the reader understand the sound being made in this sentence.

ALLITERATION

Alliteration is a stylistic device, or literary technique, in which successive words (more strictly, stressed syllables) begin with the same sound or letter. Alliteration is a frequent tool in poetry but it is also common in prose, particularly to highlight short phrases. An example of alliteration could be "thundering through the thickets," in which the initial th sound is used in four consecutive words. Especially in poetry, it contributes to euphony of the passage, lending it a musical air. It may act to humorous effect. Alliteration draws attention to itself, which may be a good or a bad thing. Authors should be conscious of the character of the sound to be repeated. In the above example, a *th* sound is somewhat difficult to make quickly in four consecutive words, so the phrase conveys a little of the difficulty of moving through tall grass. If the author is indeed trying to suggest this difficulty, then the alliteration is a success. Consider, however, the description of eyes as "glassy globes of glitter." This is definitely alliteration, since the initial *gl* sound is used three times. However, one might question whether this awkward sound is appropriate for a description of pretty eyes. The phrase is not especially pleasant to the ear, and therefore is probably not effective as alliteration. Related to alliteration are *assonance*, the repetition of vowel sounds, and *consonance*, the repetition of consonant sounds.

FIGURE OF SPEECH

A figure of speech, sometimes termed a rhetorical figure or device, or elocution, is a word or phrase that departs from straightforward, literal language. Figures of speech are often used and crafted for emphasis, freshness of expression, or clarity. However, clarity may also suffer if figures of speech are overused or wrongly used, so caution is needed.

As an example of the figurative use of a word, consider the sentence, "I am going to crown you." It may mean:

- I am going to place a literal crown on your head.
- I am going to symbolically exalt you to the place of kingship.
- I am going to punch you in the head with my clenched fist.
- I am going to put a second checker on top of your checker to signify that it has become a king.

METAPHOR

A metaphor is a type of figurative language in which the writer equates one thing with a different thing. In the sentence "The bird was an arrow arcing through the sky," the arrow is serving as a metaphor for the bird. The point of a metaphor is to encourage the reader to think about the thing being described in a different way. Using this example, we are being asked to envision the bird's flight as similar to the arc of an arrow, so we will imagine it to be swift and bending. Metaphors are a way for the author to describe without being direct and obvious. Metaphors are a more lyrical and suggestive way of providing information. Note that the thing to which a metaphor refers will not always be mentioned explicitly by the author. For instance, consider the following description of a forest in winter: "Swaying skeletons reached for the sky and groaned as the wind blew through them." The author is clearly using *skeletons* as a metaphor for leafless trees. This metaphor creates a spooky tone while inspiring the reader's imagination.

> **Review Video: <u>Metaphor</u>**
> Visit mometrix.com/academy and enter code: 133295

METONYMY

Metonymy is referring to one thing in terms of another, closely related thing. This is similar to metaphor, but there is less distance between the description and the thing being described. An example of metonymy is referring to the news media as the "press," although the press is the device by which newspapers are printed. Metonymy is a way of referring to something without having to repeat its name constantly. Synecdoche, on the other hand, is referring to a whole by one of its parts. An example of synecdoche would be calling a police officer a "badge." Synecdoche, like metonymy, is a handy way of reference without having to overuse certain words. It also allows the writer to emphasize aspects of the thing being described. For instance, referring to businessmen as "suits" suggests professionalism, conformity, and drabness.

HYPERBOLE

Hyperbole is overstatement for effect. The following sentence is an example of hyperbole: *He jumped ten feet in the air when he heard the good news*. Obviously, no person has the ability to jump ten feet in the air. The author hyperbolizes not because he believes the statement will be taken literally, but because the exaggeration conveys the extremity of emotion. Consider how much less colorful the sentence would be if the author simply said, "He jumped when he heard the good news." Hyperbole can be ineffective if the author does not exaggerate enough. For instance, if the author wrote, "He jumped two feet in the air when he heard the good news," the reader might not be sure whether this is actually true or just hyperbole. In many situations this distinction will not really matter. However, an author should avoid confusing or vague hyperbole when he needs to maintain credibility or authority with readers.

UNDERSTATEMENT

Understatement is the opposite of hyperbole. This device discounts or downplays something. Think about someone who climbs Mount Everest. Then, they say that the journey was *a little stroll*. As with other types of figurative language, understatement has a range of uses. The device may show self-defeat or modesty as in the Mount Everest example. However, some may think of understatement as false modesty (i.e., an attempt to bring attention to you or a situation). For example, a woman is praised on her diamond engagement ring. The woman says, *Oh, this little thing?* Her understatement might be heard as stuck-up or unfeeling.

> **Review Video: Hyperbole and Understatement**
> Visit mometrix.com/academy and enter code: 308470

SIMILE AND METAPHOR

A simile is a figurative expression similar to a metaphor, though it requires the use of a distancing word like *like* or *as*. Some examples are "The sun was like an orange," "eager as a beaver," and "nimble as a mountain goat." Because a simile includes *like* or a*s*, it creates a little space between the description and the thing being described. If an author says that a house was "like a shoebox," the tone is slightly different than if the author said that the house *was* a shoebox. In a simile, the author indicates an awareness that the description is not the same thing as the thing being described. In a metaphor, there is no such distinction, even though one may safely assume that the author is aware of it. This is a subtle difference, but authors will alternately use metaphors and similes depending on their intended tone.

> **Review Video: Simile**
> Visit mometrix.com/academy and enter code: 642949

PERSONIFICATION

Another type of figurative language is personification. This is the description of the nonhuman as if it were human. Literally, the word means the process of making something into a person. There is a wide range of approaches to personification, from common expressions like "whispering wind" to full novels like *Animal Farm* (George Orwell), in which the Bolshevik Revolution is reenacted by farmyard animals. The general intent of personification is to describe things in a manner that will be comprehensible to readers. When an author states that a tree "groans" in the wind, he/she of course does not mean that the tree is emitting a low, pained sound from its mouth. Instead, he/she means that the tree is making a noise similar to a human groan. This personification establishes a

tone of sadness or suffering. A different tone would be established if the author said the tree was "swaying" or "dancing."

IRONY

Irony is a statement that suggests its opposite—an author or character says one thing but means another. For example, imagine a man walks in his front door, covered in mud and in tattered clothes. His wife asks him, "How was your day?" and he says "Great!" As in this example, irony often depends on information the reader obtains elsewhere. There is a fine distinction between irony and sarcasm. Irony is any statement in which the literal meaning is opposite from the intended meaning, while sarcasm is a statement of this type that is also insulting to the person at whom it is directed. A sarcastic statement suggests that the other person is stupid enough to believe an obviously false statement is true, while irony is a bit more subtle.

Reading Comprehension Practice Test

Directions: Each passage in the reading section is followed by several questions. Choose the best answer from the choices given.

Questions 1 to 3 refer to the following passage:

> Alexander the Great died in Babylon at the age of 32 in 323 BC. He had been sick and febrile for two weeks prior to his death. Much speculation exists regarding his cause of death. Poisoning, assassination, and a number of infectious diseases have been posited. An incident mentioned by Plutarch may provide a significant clue. Shortly before his illness, as Alexander entered the city of Babylon, he was met by a flock of ravens. The birds behaved strangely, and many came to die at his feet. The strange behavior of these birds, taken as an ill omen at the time, is similar to the illness and death of birds observed in the United States in the weeks preceding the identification of the first human cases of the West Nile virus. This information suggests that Alexander the Great may have died of encephalitis caused by the West Nile virus.

1. The main purpose of this passage is to

    a. describe the symptoms of West Nile virus encephalitis.
    b. describe an incident involving birds and Alexander the Great.
    c. propose a cause for the death of Alexander the Great.
    d. connect Alexander the Great and Plutarch.

2. In the passage above, "posited" is synonymous with

    a. proposed.
    b. implicated.
    c. amplified.
    d. infected.

3. The author believes that the illness and death of birds observed in the United States indicated that the birds in Babylon

    a. were an ill omen.
    b. were ravens.
    c. were mentioned by Plutarch.
    d. were infected by the encephalitis virus.

Questions 4 to 7 refer to the following passage:

The invalidation of the Ptolemaic model of the solar system is owed chiefly to Nicolaus Copernicus, a 15th century astronomer from Poland. An early Renaissance man, Copernicus studied a wide range of subjects encompassing mathematics, astronomy, medicine, and law. He studied at the University of Krakow and later at the University of Bologna. While in Italy, his investigations led him to question the widely held belief of the time that the sun and planets revolved around the earth.

In Copernicus' time, people believed that the earth was motionless and fixed at the center of the universe. This model had originated with the Greek astronomer Ptolemy 1,000 years earlier and was supported strongly by the Catholic Church. Copernicus, a church canon himself, challenged the Ptolemaic theory. In its place, he proposed a heliocentric or sun-centered astronomic model. From his observations, made with the naked eye, Copernicus concluded that all the planets—including the earth—revolved around the sun. He also measured the earth's daily axial rotation and proposed this motion as the cause of the apparent movement of heavenly bodies. Working before the advent of the telescope, Copernicus could not prove his theories. He died in 1543.

4. Which of the following sentences best states the main premise of this passage?
- a. Copernicus was an astronomer who followed in the footsteps of Ptolemy.
- b. Copernicus's observations revolutionized astronomy in the 16th century.
- c. Copernicus concealed a heliocentric theory of astronomy.
- d. Copernicus was a bishop in the Catholic Church.

5. The passage implies that Copernicus could not prove his theories because
- a. they were wrong.
- b. they were opposed by the Catholic Church.
- c. he had no telescope.
- d. he was too busy with his work in law and medicine.

6. In the passage above, the word "heliocentric" means
- a. with the naked eye.
- b. a motionless earth.
- c. revolutionary.
- d. with the sun at the center.

7. This passage is best labeled a
- a. cause and effect essay.
- b. persuasive essay.
- c. process analysis essay.
- d. description essay.

Questions 8 to 11 refer to the following passage:

Some wine aficionados prize the flavor of oak, usually imparted to the beverage through aging in wooden barrels. An alternative process, aging in metal casks with macerated wood chips, provides a stronger wood flavor in less time and therefore is less expensive. To test consumer preferences for wines processed in this manner, a survey of 618 people living in several East Coast cities was conducted early last year. Participants took a blind taste test of three samples of Oregon Pinot Noir. One sample was aged using macerated wood chips, one sample was aged under oak, and a third sample (the control) was aged in a metal tank. A questionnaire then asked subjects to rate the wines and asked a variety of other questions aimed at categorizing the subjects' consumption habits.

Although a variety of factors influenced wine preference, the test exposed a pattern concerning a preference for strongly wood-flavored wines. A large proportion of those persons interviewed (45%) did not care for the tannic wines. However, a sizable minority of 25% especially liked them very much, and preferred the tannic wines to the other samples. Younger consumers particularly fell into this category. Connoisseurs reported greater appreciation for wines aged "under oak," or in normal oak barrels.

Many high-quality wines today are aged under oak. Nonetheless, this process is time consuming; as a result, it makes wines more expensive. This survey demonstrated that price is very important in the buying decision, especially for people without extensive knowledge regarding wine. Many consumers are more concerned with price differences than with subtle differences in flavor. This trend defines a market segment that might be well served by wines aged with wood chips.

8. The main purpose of this passage is to describe
  a. the process of aging wine with wood chips.
  b. consumer preferences in wines.
  c. the importance of price in wine marketing.
  d. a survey that tested consumer preferences.

9. The word "macerated" is closest in meaning to
  a. reduced.
  b. liquefied.
  c. persecuted.
  d. facilitated.

10. According to the passage, what percentage of respondents did not like oak-flavored wines?
  a. 75%
  b. 55%
  c. 45%
  d. 25%

11. Which of the following statements best explains the advantage of using wood chips to make wine?
- a. It is an inexpensive way of making wines that appeal to young people.
- b. It is an inexpensive way of making wines that appeal to connoisseurs.
- c. It is a faster way to make expensive wines.
- d. It makes wines that are indistinguishable from those produced by more expensive processes.

Questions 12 to 14 refer to the following passage:

The loss of barrier islands through erosion poses a serious challenge to many communities along the Atlantic and Gulf Coasts. Along with marshes and wetlands, these islands protect coastal towns from major storms. In the past seventy years, Louisiana alone has lost almost 2,000 square miles of coastal land to hurricanes and flooding. More than 100 square miles of wetlands protecting the city of New Orleans were wiped out by a single storm, Hurricane Katrina. Due to this exposure of coastal communities, recent hurricane seasons have proven the most expensive on record: annual losses since 2005 have been estimated in the hundreds of billions of dollars. This unfortunate trend is likely to continue, since meteorological research shows that the Atlantic basin is in an active storm period that could continue for decades.

12. Which of the following statements offers a supporting argument for the passage's claim that many coastal islands are eroding?
- a. Recent hurricane seasons have been expensive.
- b. The Atlantic Basin is entering an active period.
- c. Louisiana has lost 2,000 square miles of coastal land.
- d. Barrier islands are the first line of defense against coastal storms.

13. The passage describes recent hurricane seasons as the most expensive on record. Which of the following statements gives the implied reason for this increased expense?
- a. Hurricane Katrina was an extremely violent storm.
- b. Valuable buildings were destroyed in New Orleans.
- c. The Atlantic Basin is entering an active period.
- d. Destruction of barrier islands and coastal wetlands has left the mainland exposed.

14. Which of the following choices represents the best label for this passage?
- a. definition essay
- b. cause/effect essay
- c. comparison essay
- d. persuasive essay

Questions 15 and 16 refer to the following passage:

Intercity passenger rail is widely used in Europe and Japan. In the United States, it could potentially provide significant benefits to society by complementing other heavily used modes of transportation. Potential benefits include controlling increases in air and highway congestion, stemming pollution caused by aircraft and automobiles, reducing fuel consumption and energy dependency, and increasing passenger safety. Rail transport can compete in markets comprised of nearby cities as well as along routes that parallel heavily traveled highway or air corridors.

15. This passage is best described as one that
   a. advocates implementation of a passenger rail system.
   b. describes passenger rail systems.
   c. points out advantages and disadvantages of passenger rail systems.
   d. narrates a trip on a passenger rail system.

16. The author sees intercity passenger rail as
   a. a replacement for other forms of travel such as air or highway.
   b. an alternative form of travel suited to all intercity routes in the United States.
   c. lacking any advantages over currently popular forms of travel.
   d. capable of augmenting currently available forms of travel in selected markets.

Question 17 refers to the following passage:

Absurdity is required for progress. It is absurd to try to change the world.

17. In this passage,
   a. the first sentence explains the second sentence.
   b. the second sentence explains the first sentence.
   c. neither sentence is a consequence of the other sentence.
   d. the two sentences comprise a circular argument.

Questions 18 to 22 refer to the following passage:

Magnesium is an important nutrient that supports immune system functioning and helps protect the body against cardiovascular diseases. Symptoms of magnesium deficiency rarely surface among populations in developed countries, but concern is growing that many people may not have sufficient body stores of this metal. Surveys show that most Americans do not receive the minimum daily requirement of magnesium in their diets.

Magnesium is absorbed from foods by the intestines, before the circulatory system transports it to the body's tissues. Less than half of ingested magnesium is normally taken up in this way. Health issues affecting the digestive tract may impair magnesium absorption. For example, gastrointestinal disorders such as Crohn's disease can limit magnesium uptake. The kidneys normally limit urinary excretion of magnesium, a function that can help make up for low dietary intake. However, alcohol abuse and certain medications can affect this balance and thereby lead to magnesium depletion.

Symptoms of magnesium deficiency include vomiting, fatigue, and loss of appetite. More severe cases can include symptoms such as muscular cramps, seizures, and coronary abnormalities. Magnesium insufficiency also can affect the body's ability to absorb other cations, including calcium and potassium, and can lead to other health complications. Good sources of dietary magnesium include leafy green vegetables, potatoes, nuts, and seeds.

18. Which of the following statements is true?
 a. People with magnesium deficiency commonly exhibit fatigue and loss of appetite.
 b. People with magnesium deficiencies are often asymptomatic.
 c. Severe magnesium deficiency may lead to Crohn's disease.
 d. Magnesium is not absorbed by the digestive tract.

19. Which of the following labels best describes the previous passage?
 a. comparison essay
 b. definition essay
 c. cause and effect essay
 d. persuasive essay

20. Which of the following describes the intestine's normal absorption of magnesium?
 a. inefficient.
 b. very efficient except when disease is present.
 c. rarely observed among the populations of developing countries.
 d. enhanced by eating leafy green vegetables.

21. According to the passage, alcohol abuse can lead to which of the following problems?
 a. poor magnesium absorption.
 b. an impairment of kidney function.
 c. compromise of the immune system.
 d. gastrointestinal disorders.

22. The word "cation" is closest in meaning to:

a. element
b. nutrient similar to magnesium
c. symptom of deficiency
d. nutritional supplement

Questions 23 and 24 refer to the following passage:

Students may take classes in a wide variety of subjects for fun or self-improvement. Some classes provide students with training in useful life skills such as cooking or personal finance. Other classes provide instruction for recreational purposes, with topics such as photography, pottery, or painting. Classes may be large or small, or may involve one-on-one instruction in subjects like singing or playing a musical instrument. Classes taught by self-enrichment teachers seldom lead to a degree, and attendance in these classes is voluntary. Although often taught in nonacademic settings, topics may include academic subjects such as literature, foreign languages, and history. Despite their informal nature, these courses can provide students with useful, work-related skills such as knowledge of computers or foreign languages; these skills can make students more attractive to potential employers.

23. Which of the following statements represents the central idea of this passage?

a. Self-improvement classes teach work-related skills.
b. Attendance is voluntary for self-improvement classes.
c. Many different kinds of self-improvement classes are available.
d. Cooking is one type of self-improvement classes.

24. Which of the following statements is true?

a. All self-improvement classes offer training in recreational subject areas.
b. Self-improvement classes usually are taught in non-academic settings.
c. Some informal classes teach useful work-related skills.
d. In order to learn a foreign language, a student must enroll in a formal, degree-granting program.

Questions 25 and 26 refer to the following passage:

The makeup she applied, although intended to display her pulchritude, instead revealed her narcissism.

25. In the context of this sentence, the word "pulchritude" means

a. beauty
b. dexterity
c. skill
d. sense of color

26. A synonym for the word "narcissism," as used in the text, is

a. superiority
b. respect
c. conceitedness
d. timidity

Questions 27 to 30 refer to the following passage:

The selection of trees for planting in urban areas poses severe challenges due to soil adversities and space restrictions both above and belowground. Restricted spaces, especially in "downtown" situations or in densely built neighborhoods, make selecting, planting, and managing trees in urban areas difficult. Urban sites pose adversities that severely constrain the palette of suitable trees. As a result, an urgent need exists to find tough, small species of trees for urban spaces. Dwarf forms of native species have not been utilized greatly, and some foreign species may prove to be appropriate.

27. Which of the following is NOT identified by the passage as a problem encountered when planting trees in urban sites?
   a. poor soil
   b. air pollution
   c. limited room for root development
   d. restricted space

28. In the context of this passage, the word "palette" means
   a. a board used by painters for mixing colors.
   b. choice.
   c. wooden platform.
   d. repertoire.

29. In the last sentence, which of the following statements does the author imply regarding dwarf forms of native species, which have not been greatly utilized?
   a. They are too small.
   b. They are ill-suited to urban sites.
   c. They would do better in foreign locations.
   d. They would do well in urban sites.

30. This passage is best described as a
   a. problem/solution essay.
   b. cause/effect essay.
   c. persuasive essay.
   d. narration essay.

Questions 31 to 33 refer to the following passage:

A new way to circumvent the cost and limitations of long distance telephone is called Voice over Internet Protocol, or VoIP. VoIP sends digital information over the Internet to the person you are calling. The information may come from your phone or your computer, and may comprise both voice and video signal if you have a camera. Companies that specialize in such technology as well as some traditional phone companies offer VoIP services. Some services require that you call from a computer augmented by special software, a microphone, speakers, and a sound card. Other services allow you to call from any regular phone without special equipment.

31. The word "circumvent" is closest in meaning to

    a. reduce.
    b. magnify.
    c. elude.
    d. camouflage.

32. Which of the following is required to take advantage of VoIP services?

    a. a camera
    b. a telephone
    c. special software
    d. none of the above

33. The information in the passage best supports which of the following statements?

    a. Voice over Internet Protocol services are available in most telephone markets.
    b. Voice over Internet Protocol services digitally encode voice and visual information.
    c. Voice over Internet Protocol services provide higher quality signals than traditional telephone services.
    d. Voice over Internet Protocol services must be purchased from companies that specialize in the technology.

Questions 34 to 37 refer to the following passage:

The provision of this bill that prevents any nonprofit recipient of a housing grant from conducting voter registration is an outrageous, undemocratic amendment that imposes restrictions on promoting the most fundamental of our civil liberties, the right to vote. This provision forbids any nonprofits from even applying for a grant if they have encouraged voting in the recent past. Restricting the prerogatives of nonprofits in this way is a violation of the first amendment rights of these organizations. There is absolutely no justification for preventing the efforts of nonprofit organizations to encourage civic activities such as voting.

34. This passage is best described as a

    a. problem/solution essay.
    b. cause/effect essay.
    c. persuasive essay.
    d. narration essay.

35. The word "prerogative" is closest in meaning to

a. privilege.
b. funding.
c. restriction.
d. ability.

36. What is the author's tone?

a. entertaining
b. angry
c. informative
d. apologetic

37. What is the author's main argument against the provision?

a. It will prevent voting.
b. It is unconstitutional.
c. It will prevent nonprofit organizations from receiving funding.
d. It is unjustified.

Questions 38 to 40 refer to the following passage:

Women have made significant contributions to patent literature in fields as diverse as domestic technology and biomedicine. A woman was involved in the design of the first computer: Lady Ada Lovelace worked with Charles Babbage to build the "difference engine," a device that could add and subtract. More recently, Gertrude Elion won the 1988 Nobel Prize in Medicine for her invention of a leukemia treatment based on immunosuppressants. She holds numerous medical patents. In addition, women have served as leading members of teams developing surgical methods and all the current AIDS drugs.

38. The "difference engine" was

a. domestic technology.
b. a device used in biomedicine.
c. a computer.
d. invented by Gertrude Elion.

39. The structure of this paragraph is best described as

a. topic sentence and analysis
b. topic sentence and consequences
c. introductory sentence followed by causes and reasons
d. topic sentence followed by examples

40. The passage implies that

a. women are more productive inventors than men.
b. many surgical methods are patented.
c. women's contributions to the patent literature have been underappreciated.
d. Gertrud Elion did not deserve the Nobel Prize.

Reading Comprehension Answers and Explanations

1. C: Although the passage does describe some of the symptoms of encephalitis caused by the West Nile virus as well as the incident in which the birds died at Alexander's feet; these descriptions are incidental to the paragraph's main purpose. The main idea of the paragraph is that Alexander may have died of encephalitis.

2. A: The third sentence, in which this word appears, reviews a number of possible, suggested, or proposed causes for Alexander's death. The author then recounts the incident of the ravens as evidence for a different cause of death.

3. D: The author's thesis holds that the birds contracted the encephalitis virus first and that it led to their death. The virus then spread to the human population, leading to the outbreak of West Nile encephalitis. The author suggests that this train of events occurred both in ancient Babylon and in the modern United States.

4. B: The passage describes how Copernicus made observations that contradicted the prevailing view of astronomy, which had been held since the time of Ptolemy. The Ptolemaic theory asserted that the sun and other planets revolved around the earth. The passage states that Copernicus came to question the Ptolemaic theory and challenged it. He did not conceal a heliocentric theory (Choice C), but rather propounded one.

5. C: The second paragraph in the passage states that Copernicus made his observations with the naked eye. The penultimate sentence states that he worked before the advent of the telescope and that he could not prove his theories. The paragraph implies that a telescope would have made this proof possible.

6. D: The third sentence of the second paragraph states that Copernicus put forward the principles of a "heliocentric or sun-centered astronomy," in which the sun was at the center of rotation of the orbiting planets.

7. D: The essay describes the history of Copernicus and his astronomical observations, telling the reader about his life and contrasting his astronomical observations to those previously made by the ancient Greeks. It does not seek to persuade or to promote a particular point of view. It does not describe or analyze a process or describe any cause-and-effect relationships.

8. D: Although the passage describes various methods of aging wine in the presence of oak as well as consumer price sensitivity, the passage's main purpose is to describe the results of a survey conducted in order to examine consumer preferences. The passage describes the number of people surveyed, the types of questions asked, and the results of the survey.

9. A: To macerate is to break into smaller parts, typically by steeping in a liquid. In this case, the process produces small wood chips with a large surface area that flavors the wine more efficiently than the interior surface of the barrels used traditionally.

10. C: The second paragraph states that 45% of those persons interviewed rejected tannic wines. Tannic wines are those flavored by tannins, components of oak bark. The meaning of the term can be inferred from the phrasing of the second paragraph, in which the 25% who strongly favored the wood-flavored wines are contrasted to those who categorically disliked the tannic wines.

11. A: The second paragraph states that young wine lovers, especially, fell into the 25% who preferred the wood-chip produced wines. The first paragraph states that the process is faster and therefore less expensive. Additionally, the last paragraph indicates that price sensitivity among consumers is an advantage for wines made with wood chips, from which one may infer that the process is less expensive.

12. C: The loss of coastal wetlands in Louisiana is an example of coastal island erosion caused by hurricanes, and so supports the statement. The other choices are also statements that appear in the passage, but they do not provide direct support for the claim that many coastal islands are eroding.

13. D: The passage describes the loss of these coastal barrier lands to erosion. The fifth sentence then states, "the result is that recent hurricane seasons have been the most expensive on record." This establishes the cause-and-effect between barrier island erosion and monetary losses due to great storms.

14. B: The essay does not make comparisons or seek to define or persuade. Instead, this passage describes the role of coastal wetlands, gives examples of recent losses of these lands, and concludes that these factors result in a substantial economic loss due to recent storms.

15. A: By pointing out only the benefits of a passenger rail system, the author attempts to make the case for the implementation of such a system in the United States. The author does not offer a description of the equipment or procedures used by such a system, but instead enumerates its advantages.

16. D: The author states that rail can complement other heavily used forms of transportation, including heavily traveled corridors between cities within close distances.

17. B: The logic of the passage holds that 1) trying to change the world is absurd; 2) progress changes the world; and therefore, 3) absurdity is required for progress.

18. B: The first paragraph indicates that symptoms of magnesium deficiency rarely are observed, but a concern exists that people may have insufficient stores of this nutrient.

19. C: The passage describes both the causes of magnesium deficiency (dietary shortage or poor uptake exacerbated by gastrointestinal disorders) and its results (reduced functioning of the immune system and lessened resistance to cardiovascular disease).

20. A: The second paragraph informs that less than half of ingested magnesium is absorbed under normal circumstances.

21. B: According to the second paragraph, the kidneys usually limit magnesium excretion in the urine, but alcohol abuse and/or certain medications may affect this function. Impairment of this kidney function may lead to magnesium depletion. The passage does not state that magnesium uptake—a function of the intestines—is affected by alcohol.

22. B: The final paragraph indicates that magnesium deficiency can affect the absorption of "other cations," implying that magnesium itself is also a cation. The examples given, calcium and potassium, are also nutrients.

23. C: The passage explores the wide variety of self-improvement classes offered. As such, it touches upon the variety of content and subject matter, different venues in which the classes may be taught, and the range of enrollment sizes that may be encountered.

24. C: The passage points out that some of the subjects taught in informal courses may prove useful in the workplace and may make the student more desirable to potential employers. This includes topics such as computer science and foreign languages.

25. A: Pulchritude means "beauty," and in this case refers to the method of putting on makeup to enhance natural beauty.

26. C: The word "narcissism" comes from the name of the Greek god Narcissus, who was so attractive that he enjoyed gazing at his reflection in a pond. Narcissism refers to excessive fascination with oneself, one's appearance, etc.

27. B: The first sentence identifies poor soil as a problem in the first sentence ("soil adversities"). The second sentence points to restricted space, both above and belowground (the latter restricting root development). Although air pollution also may affect the growth of urban trees, the passage does not mention this factor.

28. D: The word, derived from the board used by painters during the Renaissance, refers to the variety of techniques or materials available in any art. The third sentence of the passage informs us that this range is limited by the adverse conditions in urban sites. Note that the word refers to the range of available trees, and not to the choice made among them, so Choice B is incorrect.

29. D: Since space restriction is one of the major problems encountered in planting trees in urban sites, the author implies that dwarf trees—since they are small—would prove successful in this cramped environment.

30. A: The essay first poses a problem—namely, the difficulty of growing trees in urban environments due to poor soil and limited space. The author then suggests two solutions to this problem: dwarf trees, which are small and require limited space, and foreign species, which are less well known and may include some particularly hardy examples.

31. C: To "circumvent" means to get around an obstacle or problem or to find a way to avoid it. To "elude" has the same meaning. The problem in this case is one of high cost, and circumventing it leads to a reduction in that cost, as in Choice A. Nevertheless, Choice C is the closest in meaning.

32. D: Although certain circumstances might require each of the choices, the article makes a point of enumerating the variety of providers available and that different equipment configurations will work with different services. This includes computer-based and telephone-based services.

33. B: The second sentence defines VoIP as something that uses the internet to send digital information. The third sentence specifies that this information may comprise both voice and video signals. Although digital VoIP signals may be of higher quality than other technologies and may be available in most markets, the passage does not make these points.

34. C: The passage is an argument against a legislative proposal. Its purpose is to persuade legislators or voters to reject the proposal or the provision it discusses. The tone of the passage is contentious and opinionated, not objective like narrative writing. It does not attempt to present an opposing point of view or an analysis, as would befit cause/effect or problem/solution writing.

35. A: A prerogative is a right or privilege, in this case the right to conduct voter registration activities.

36. B: The author plainly is not attempting to entertain. The use of words such as "outrageous," "undemocratic," and "absolutely" imparts a strongly emotional tone to the passage, which can be described as antagonistic, irate, or angry.

37. B: In the third sentence, the author argues that the provision violates the first amendment of the Constitution. Although the passage also claims such a provision as unjustified, this claim offers not so much an argument as a rhetorical flourish.

38. C: The introductory phrase of the second sentence, "A woman was involved in the design of the first computer:" ends with a colon, indicating that an example will follow. Thus, the difference engine described in the following clause is an example of a computer. The difference engine is described further in the passage as a device that could add and subtract, which is a function of a computer.

39. D: The first sentence introduces the topic, the contributions made to the patent literature by women. The remainder of the paragraph is dedicated to giving examples of these contributions, beginning with Lady Lovelace two centuries ago and continuing through present day contributions to biomedicine. The passage does not describe any causes or effects, so the passage cannot be considered an analysis.

40. B: The thrust of the paragraph asserts that women have registered many patents. The final sentence informs us that women have led teams that developed surgical methods. Although not stated explicitly, the paragraph implies that these methods have been patented.

Mathematics

In the high tech world we live in, it might seem that having good math ability is no longer very important. After all, when does a person have to mentally perform even the easiest math operation anymore? It seems that any time you need to deal with math, the work has already been done for you, or you simply have to push a few buttons on a computer, smart phone, or—if you're really old-fashioned—on an actual calculator.

It's true that there has been quite a revolution when it comes to how we do math even in the last 10–20 years. As hard as it may be to believe today, when small, portable calculators first came on the American market around 1970, they cost about $300 (about $1800 in today's dollars!) and performed only the four basic functions—addition, subtraction, division, and multiplication. Very few people could afford to own one, and most people still used pencil and paper to solve math problems. Now you can buy a better calculator for about a dollar at most discount stores.

If you're like the average person, though, it's been a long time since you used an actual handheld calculator, let alone pencil and paper, to solve any math problems. You use your phone or computer to do math on the rare occasions when it comes up. When those first portable calculators came out, many people predicted that one day in the not too distant future math knowledge would become superfluous for the average person. It might seem as if their prediction came true.

Yet while math may have become superfluous in the day-to-day lives of most people, math abilities are still essential for success in life. We may use different tools to perform our "figuring" these days, but it's still vital to know how to do the operations ourselves. A person with a well-rounded education should be able to perform all but the most complicated math operations either mentally or with pencil and paper.

This is why civil service exams have math questions. An office worker shouldn't need to stop and open up the computer's calculator function every time he needs to add, subtract, multiply or divide. He/she should be able to do basic math mentally. So, in order to do well on your civil service exam, you'll need to make sure your math knowledge and skills are in good shape. If you've been out of school for several years, your skills might have gotten a little rusty, and you may not be as familiar with some of the more advanced or less frequently used concepts as you once were.

In this chapter you'll find a thorough refresher course in math to get you up to speed quickly. It starts with the basics and then builds on that foundation all the way through algebra and geometry. (Yes, you may very well encounter basic algebra or geometry questions, or both, on the civil service test.) Even if you struggled with math in school, you'll find all the information you need to master the math portion of the civil service exam in this chapter. Take your time and go at your own pace, and use the practice test at the end as a diagnostic tool to measure your readiness for the exam.

NUMBERS AND THEIR CLASSIFICATIONS

Numbers are the basic building blocks of mathematics. Specific features of numbers are identified by the following terms:

- Integers—the set of whole positive and negative numbers, including zero. Integers do not include fractions ($\frac{1}{3}$), decimals (0.56), or mixed numbers ($7\frac{3}{4}$).
- Prime number—a whole number greater than 1 that has only two factors, itself and 1. An example is 11, which is only divisible by 1 and 11. However, 1 itself is not a prime number since it has only one factor, 1.
- Composite number—a whole number greater than 1 that has more than two factors; in other words, any whole number that is not a prime number. For example, the composite number 8 has the factors of 1, 2, 4, and 8.
- Even number—any integer that can be divided by 2 without leaving a remainder. The integers 2, 4, 6, 8, and so on are even numbers.
- Odd number—any integer that cannot be divided evenly by 2. The integers 3, 5, 7, 9, and so on are odd numbers.
- Decimal number—a non-integer that uses a decimal point to show the part of the number that is less than one. An example of a decimal number is 1.234.
- Decimal point—a symbol used to separate the ones place from the tenths place in decimals or dollars from cents in currency.
- Decimal place—the position of a number to the right of the decimal point. In the decimal 0.123, the 1 is in the first place to the right of the decimal point, indicating tenths; the 2 is in the second place, indicating hundredths; and the 3 is in the third place, indicating thousandths.

The decimal, or base 10, system is a number system that uses ten different digits (0, 1, 2, 3, 4, 5, 6, 7, 8, 9). An example of a number system that uses something other than ten digits is the binary, or base 2, number system, used by computers, which uses only the numbers 0 and 1. It is thought that the decimal system originated because people used their 10 fingers for counting.

Rational, irrational, and real numbers can be described as follows:

- Rational numbers include all integers, decimals, and fractions. Any terminating or repeating decimal number is a rational number.
- Irrational numbers cannot be written as fractions or decimals because the number of decimal places is infinite and there is no recurring pattern of digits within the number. For example, pi (π) begins with 3.141592 and continues without terminating or repeating, so pi is an irrational number.
- Real numbers are the set of all rational and irrational numbers.

OPERATIONS

There are four basic mathematical operations:

- Addition increases the value of one quantity by the value of another quantity. For example, $2 + 4 = 6$; $8 + 9 = 17$. The result is called the sum. With addition, the order does not matter: $4 + 2 = 2 + 4$.
- Subtraction is the opposite operation to addition; it decreases the value of one quantity by the value of another quantity. For example, $6 - 4 = 2$; $17 - 8 = 9$. The result is called the difference. With subtraction, the order does matter: $6 - 4 \neq 4 - 6$.

122

- Multiplication can be thought of as repeated addition. One number tells how many times to add the other number to itself. For example, 3×2 (three times two) $= 2 + 2 + 2 = 6$. With multiplication, the order does not matter: $2 \times 3 = 3 \times 2$ or $3 + 3 = 2 + 2 + 2$.
- Division is the opposite operation to multiplication; one number tells us how many parts to divide the other number into. For example, $20 \div 4 = 5$; 20 can be split into 4 equal parts of 5. With division, the order of the numbers does matter: $20 \div 4 \neq 4 \div 20$.

EXPONENTS

An exponent is a superscript number placed at the top right of another number. It indicates how many times the base number is to be multiplied by itself. Exponents provide a shorthand way to write what would be a longer mathematical expression. For example, $a^2 = a \times a$; $2^4 = 2 \times 2 \times 2 \times 2$. A number with an exponent of 2 is said to be "squared," while a number with an exponent of 3 is said to be "cubed." The value of a number raised to an exponent is called its power. So, 8^4 is read as "8 to the 4th power," or "8 raised to the power of 4." A negative exponent is the same as the reciprocal of a positive exponent. For example, $a^{-2} = \frac{1}{a^2}$.

The laws of exponents are as follows:

- Any number to the power of 1 is equal to itself: $a^1 = a$.
- The number 1 raised to any power is 1: $1^n = 1$.
- Any number raised to the power of 0 is 1: $a^0 = 1$.
- Add exponents to multiply powers of the same base number: $a^n \times a^m = a^{n+m}$.
- Subtract exponents to divide powers of the same number: $a^n \div a^m = a^{n-m}$.
- Multiply exponents to raise a power to a power: $(a^n)^m = a^{n \times m}$.
- If multiplied or divided numbers inside parentheses are collectively raised to a power, this is the same as each individual term being raised to that power: $(a \times b)^n = a^n \times b^n$; $(a \div b)^n = a^n \div b^n$.

Exponents do not have to be integers. Fractional or decimal exponents follow all the rules above as well. Example: $5^{\frac{1}{4}} \times 5^{\frac{3}{4}} = 5^{\frac{1}{4}+\frac{3}{4}} = 5^1 = 5$.

A root, such as a square root, is another way of writing a fractional exponent. Instead of using a superscript, roots use the radical symbol ($\sqrt{}$) to indicate the operation. A radical has a number underneath the bar, and may sometimes also have a number in the upper left: $\sqrt[n]{a}$, read as "the nth root of a." The relationship between radical notation and exponent notation can be described by this equation: $\sqrt[n]{a} = a^{\frac{1}{n}}$. The two special cases of $n = 2$ and $n = 3$ are called square roots and cube roots. If there is no number to the upper left, it is understood to be a square root ($n = 2$). Nearly all of the roots you encounter will be square roots. A square root is the same as a number raised to the one-half power. When we say that a is the square root of b ($a = \sqrt{b}$), we mean that a multiplied by itself equals b: ($a \times a = b$).

PARENTHESES

Parentheses are used to designate which operations should be done first in equations with multiple operations. For example, $4 - (2 + 1) = 1$; the parentheses tell us that we must first add 2 and 1, and then subtract the sum from 4, rather than simply moving from left to right: $4 - 2 + 1 = 3$.

ORDER OF OPERATIONS

Order of operations is a set of rules that dictates the order in which we must perform each operation in an expression. If an expression includes multiple different operations, the order of

123

operations tells us which to do first. The best way to remember the order of operations is to use the acronym PEMDAS, or "Please Excuse My Dear Aunt Sally." PEMDAS stands for Parentheses, Exponents, Multiplication, Division, Addition, Subtraction. It is important to understand that multiplication and division have equal precedence, as do addition and subtraction, so those pairs of operations are simply worked from left to right in order.

Example: Evaluate the expression $5 + 20 \div 4 \times (2 + 3)^2 - 6$ using the correct order of operations.

P—perform the operations inside the parentheses: $(2 + 3) = 5$.

The equation now looks like this: $5 + 20 \div 4 \times 5^2 - 6$.

E—simplify the exponents: $(5)^2 = 25$.

The equation now looks like this: $5 + 20 \div 4 \times 25 - 6$.

MD—perform multiplication and division from left to right: $20 \div 4 = 5$; $5 \times 25 = 125$.

The equation now looks like this: $5 + 125 - 6$.

AS—perform addition and subtraction from left to right: $5 + 125 = 130$; $130 - 6 = 124$.

PERFECT SQUARE

A perfect square is a number that has an integer for its square root. There are 10 perfect squares from 1 to 100: 1, 4, 9, 16, 25, 36, 49, 64, 81, 100 (the squares of integers 1 through 10).

SCIENTIFIC NOTATION

Scientific notation is a way of writing large numbers in a shorter form. The form $a \times 10^n$ is used in scientific notation, where a is greater than or equal to 1 but less than 10, and n is the number of places the decimal must move to get from the original number to a. Example: The number 230,400,000 is cumbersome to write. To write the value in scientific notation, place a decimal point between the first and second numbers, and include all digits through the last non-zero digit ($a = 2.304$). To find the appropriate power of 10, count the number of places the decimal point had to move ($n = 8$). The number is positive if the decimal moved to the left, and negative if it moved to the right. We can then write 230,400,000 as 2.304×10^8. If we look instead at the number 0.00002304, we have the same value for a, but this time the decimal moved 5 places to the right ($n = -5$). Thus, 0.00002304 can be written as 2.304×10^{-5}. Using this notation makes it simple to compare very large or very small numbers. By comparing exponents, it is easy to see that 3.28×10^4 is smaller than 1.51×10^5, because 4 is less than 5.

> **Review Video: Scientific Notation**
> Visit mometrix.com/academy and enter code: 976454

FACTORS AND MULTIPLES

Factors are numbers that are multiplied together to obtain a product. For example, in the equation $2 \times 3 = 6$, the numbers 2 and 3 are factors and 6 is the product. A prime number has only two factors (1 and itself), but other numbers can have many factors. A common factor is a number that can divide into two or more other numbers. For example, the factors of 12 are 1, 2, 3, 4, 6, and 12, while the factors of 15 are 1, 3, 5, and 15. The common factors of 12 and 15 are 1 and 3. A prime factor is a prime number that divides into another number. The prime factors of 12 are 2 and 3. For 15, the prime factors are 3 and 5. The greatest common factor (GCF) is the largest number that is a factor of two or more numbers. For example, the factors of 15 are 1, 3, 5, and 15; the factors of 35 are 1, 5, 7, and 35. Therefore, the greatest common factor of 15 and 35 is 5. The least common multiple (LCM) is the smallest number that is a multiple of two or more numbers. For example, the multiples of 3 include 3, 6, 9, 12, 15, etc.; the multiples of 5 include 5, 10, 15, 20, etc. Therefore, the least common multiple of 3 and 5 is 15.

FRACTIONS, PERCENTAGES, AND RELATED CONCEPTS
FRACTIONS

A fraction is a number expressed as one integer written above another integer, with a dividing line between them $\left(\frac{x}{y}\right)$. It represents the quotient of the two numbers: x divided by y. It can also be thought of as x out of y equal parts. The top number of a fraction is called the numerator, and it represents the number of parts under consideration. The 1 in $\frac{1}{4}$ means that 1 part out of the whole is being considered in the calculation. The bottom number of a fraction is called the denominator, and it represents the total number of equal parts. The 4 in $\frac{1}{4}$ means that the whole consists of 4 equal parts. A fraction cannot have a denominator of zero; this is referred to as "undefined."

Fractions can be manipulated without changing their value by multiplying or dividing (but not adding or subtracting) both the numerator and denominator by the same number. For example, $\frac{1}{2} \times \frac{2}{2} = \frac{2}{4}$. If you divide both numbers by a common factor, you are reducing or simplifying the fraction. Two fractions that have the same value but are expressed differently are known as equivalent fractions. For example, $\frac{2}{10}, \frac{3}{15}, \frac{4}{20}$, and $\frac{5}{25}$ are all equivalent fractions. They can also all be reduced or simplified to $\frac{1}{5}$.

When two fractions are manipulated so that they have the same denominator, this is known as finding a common denominator. The number chosen to be that common denominator should be the least common multiple of the two original denominators. For example, if you want to add $\frac{3}{4}$ and $\frac{5}{6}$, you must first find the common denominator. The least common multiple of 4 and 6 is 12. Manipulating to achieve the common denominator: $\frac{3}{4} \times \frac{3}{3} = \frac{9}{12}; \frac{5}{6} \times \frac{2}{2} = \frac{10}{12}$.

If two fractions have a common denominator, they can be added or subtracted simply by adding or subtracting the two numerators and retaining the same denominator. If the two fractions do not already have the same denominator, one or both of them must be manipulated to achieve a common denominator before they can be added or subtracted. For example: $\frac{1}{2} + \frac{1}{4} = \frac{2}{4} + \frac{1}{4} = \frac{3}{4}$.

Two fractions can be multiplied by multiplying the two numerators to find the new numerator and the two denominators to find the new denominator. For example: $\frac{1}{3} \times \frac{2}{3} = \frac{1 \times 2}{3 \times 3} = \frac{2}{9}$.

Two fractions can be divided by flipping the numerator and denominator of the second fraction and then proceeding as though it were a multiplication problem. For example: $\frac{2}{3} \div \frac{3}{4} = \frac{2}{3} \times \frac{4}{3} = \frac{8}{9}$.

A fraction whose denominator is greater than its numerator is known as a proper fraction, while a fraction whose numerator is greater than its denominator is known as an improper fraction. Proper fractions have values less than one and improper fractions have values greater than one.

MIXED NUMBERS

A mixed number contains both an integer and a fraction. Any improper fraction can be rewritten as a mixed number. For example, $\frac{8}{3} = \frac{6}{3} + \frac{2}{3} = 2 + \frac{2}{3} = 2\frac{2}{3}$. Similarly, any mixed number can be rewritten as an improper fraction. For example: $1\frac{3}{5} = 1 + \frac{3}{5} = \frac{5}{5} + \frac{3}{5} = \frac{8}{5}$.

PERCENTAGES

Percentages can be thought of as fractions that are based on a whole of 100 instead of 1; that is, one whole is equal to 100%. The word percent means "per hundred." Fractions can be expressed as percentages by finding equivalent fractions with a denomination of 100. For example: $\frac{7}{10} = \frac{70}{100} = 70\%$; $\frac{1}{4} = \frac{25}{100} = 25\%$.

To express a percentage as a fraction, divide by 100 and reduce the fraction to its simplest possible terms. For example: $60\% = \frac{60}{100} = \frac{3}{5}$; $96\% = \frac{96}{100} = \frac{24}{25}$.

Converting decimals to percentages and percentages to decimals is as simple as moving the decimal point. To convert from a decimal to a percent, move the decimal point two places to the right. To convert from a percent to a decimal, move it two places to the left. For example, 0.23 = 23%; 5.34 = 534%; 0.007 = 0.7%; 700% = 7.00; 86% = 0.86; 0.15% = 0.0015.

It may be helpful to remember that the percentage number will always be greater than the equivalent decimal number.

A percentage problem can be presented three main ways: (1) Find what percentage of some number another number is. Example: What percentage of 40 is 8? (2) Find what number is some percentage of a given number. Example: What number is 20% of 40? (3) Find what number another number is a given percentage of. Example: 8 is 20% of what number? The three components in all of these cases are the same: a whole (W), a part (P), and a percentage (%). These are related by the following equation: $P = W \times \%$. This is the form of the equation you would use to solve problems of type (2). To solve types (1) and (3), you would use these two forms: $\% = \frac{P}{W}$ and $W = \frac{P}{\%}$.

The thing that frequently makes percentage problems difficult is that they are typically word problems, so a large part of solving them is figuring out which quantities are W, P, and %. For example: In a school cafeteria, 7 students choose pizza, 9 choose hamburgers, and 4 choose tacos. Find the percentage that chooses tacos. To find the whole, you must first add all of the parts: 7 + 9 + 4 = 20. The percentage can then be found by dividing the part by the whole: $\% = \frac{P}{W}$; $\frac{4}{20} = \frac{20}{100} = 20\%$.

RATIO

A ratio is a comparison of two quantities in a particular order. For example: If there are 14 computers in a lab, and the class has 20 students, there is a student to computer ratio of 20 to 14, commonly written as 20:14. Ratios are normally reduced to their smallest whole number representation, so 20:14 would be reduced to 10:7 by dividing both sides by 2.

PROPORTION

A proportion is a relationship between two quantities that dictates how one changes when the other changes. A direct proportion describes a relationship in which a quantity increases by a set multiple for every increase in the other quantity, or decreases by that same amount for every decrease in the other quantity. Example: Assuming a constant driving speed, the time required for a

126

car trip increases as the distance of the trip increases. The distance to be traveled and the time required to travel are directly proportional.

Inverse proportion is a relationship in which an increase in one quantity is accompanied by a decrease in the other, or vice versa. Example: the time required for a car trip decreases as the speed increases, and increases as the speed decreases, so the time required is inversely proportional to the speed of the car.

DATA ANALYSIS
STATISTICS

Statistics is the branch of mathematics that deals with collecting, recording, interpreting, illustrating, and analyzing large amounts of data. The following terms are often used in the discussion of data and statistics:

- Data—the collective name for pieces of information (singular is datum).
- Quantitative data—measurements (such as length, mass, and speed) that provide information about quantities in numbers.
- Qualitative data—information (such as colors, scents, tastes, and shapes) that cannot be measured using numbers.
- Discrete data—information that can be expressed only by a specific value, such as whole or half numbers. For example, since people can be counted only in whole numbers, a population count would be discrete data.
- Continuous data—information (such as time and temperature) that can be expressed by any value within a given range.
- Primary data—information that has been collected directly from a survey, investigation, or experiment, such as a questionnaire or the recording of daily temperatures. Primary data that has not yet been organized or analyzed is called raw data.
- Secondary data—information that has been collected, sorted, and processed by the researcher.
- Ordinal data—information that can be placed in numerical order, such as age or weight.
- Nominal data—information that cannot be placed in numerical order, such as names or places.

MEASURES OF CENTRAL TENDENCY

The quantities of mean, median, and mode are all referred to as measures of central tendency. They can each give a picture of what the whole set of data looks like with just a single number. Knowing what each of these values represents is vital to making use of the information they provide. The mean, also known as the arithmetic mean or average, of a data set is calculated by summing all of the values in the set and dividing that sum by the number of values. For example, if a data set has 6 numbers and the sum of those 6 numbers is 30, the mean is calculated as 30 ÷ 6 = 5. The median is the middle value of a data set when all values are in numerical order. In the data set (1, 2, 3, 4, 5), the median is 3. If there is an even number of values in the set, the median is calculated by taking the average of the two middle values. In the data set (1, 2, 3, 4, 5, 6), the median would be (3 + 4) ÷ 2 = 3.5. The mode is the value that appears most frequently in the data set. In the data set (1, 2, 3, 4, 5, 5, 5), the mode would be 5 since this value appears three times. If multiple values appear the same number of times, there are multiple values for the mode. If the data set were (1, 2, 2, 3, 4, 4, 5, 5), the modes would be 2, 4, and 5. If no value appears more than any other value in the data set, then there is no mode.

MEASURES OF DISPERSION

The standard deviation expresses how spread out the values of a distribution are from the mean. Standard deviation is given in the same units as the original data and is represented by a lower-case sigma (σ). A high standard deviation means that the values are very spread out. A low standard deviation means that the values are close together. If every value in a distribution is increased or decreased by the same amount, the mean, median, and mode are increased or decreased by that amount, but the standard deviation stays the same. If every value in a distribution is multiplied or divided by the same number, the mean, median, mode, and standard deviation are all multiplied or divided by that number.

RANGE OF DISTRIBUTION

The range of a distribution is the difference between the highest and lowest values in the distribution. For example, in the data set (1, 3, 5, 7, 9, 11), the highest and lowest values are 11 and 1, respectively. The range would then be calculated: 11 – 1 = 10.

THREE QUARTILES

The three quartiles are the three values that divide a data set into four equal parts. Quartiles are generally only calculated for data sets with a large number of values. As a simple example, for the data set consisting of the numbers 1 through 99, the first quartile (Q1) would be 25, the second quartile (Q2), always equal to the median, would be 50, and the third quartile (Q3) would be 75. The difference between Q1 and Q3 is known as the interquartile range.

PROBABILITY

Probability is a branch of statistics that deals with the likelihood of something taking place. One classic example is a coin toss. There are only two possible results: heads or tails. The likelihood, or probability, that the coin will land as heads is 1 out of 2 (1/2, 0.5, 50%). Tails has the same probability. Another common example is a 6-sided die roll. There are six possible results from rolling a single die, each with an equal chance of happening, so the probability of any given number coming up is 1 out of 6.

Terms frequently used in probability:

- Event—a situation that produces results of some sort (such as a coin toss).
- Compound event—an event that involves two or more items (rolling a pair of dice; taking the sum).
- Outcome—a possible result in an experiment or event (heads, tails).
- Desired outcome (or success)—an outcome that meets a particular set of criteria (a roll of 1 or 2 if a number less than 3 is needed).
- Independent events—two or more events whose outcomes do not affect one another (two coins tossed at the same time).
- Dependent events—two or more events whose outcomes affect one another (two cards drawn consecutively from the same deck).
- Certain outcome—probability of outcome is 100% or 1.
- Impossible outcome—probability of outcome is 0% or 0.
- Mutually exclusive outcomes—two or more outcomes whose criteria cannot all be satisfied in a single event (a coin coming up heads and tails on the same toss).

Theoretical probability can usually be determined without actually performing the event. The likelihood of an outcome occurring, or the probability of an outcome occurring, is given by the formula:

$$P(A) = \frac{\text{Number of acceptable outcomes}}{\text{Number of possible outcomes}}$$

Note that $P(A)$ is the probability of an outcome A occurring, and each outcome is just as likely to occur as any other outcome. If each outcome has the same probability of occurring as every other possible outcome, the outcomes are said to be equally likely to occur. The total number of acceptable outcomes must be less than or equal to the total number of possible outcomes. If the two are equal, then the outcome is certain to occur and the probability is 1. If the number of acceptable outcomes is zero, then the outcome is impossible and the probability is 0. For example, if there are 20 marbles in a bag and 5 are red, then the theoretical probability of randomly selecting a red marble is 5 out of 20, ($\frac{5}{20} = \frac{1}{4}$, 0.25, or 25%).

PERMUTATIONS AND COMBINATIONS

When trying to calculate the probability of an event using the (desired outcomes)/(total outcomes) formula, you may frequently find that there are too many outcomes to individually count them. Permutation and combination formulas offer a shortcut to counting outcomes. The primary distinction between permutations and combinations is that permutations take into account order, while combinations do not. To calculate the number of possible groupings, there are two necessary parameters: the number of items available for selection and the number to be selected. The number of permutations of r items given a set of n items can be calculated as $_nP_r = \frac{n!}{(n-r)!}$. The number of combinations of r items given a set of n items can be calculated as $_nC_r = \frac{n!}{r!(n-r)!}$ or $_nC_r = \frac{_nP_r}{r!}$. For example: Suppose you want to calculate how many different 5-card hands can be drawn from a deck of 52 cards. This is a combination since the order of the cards in a hand does not matter. There are 52 cards available, and 5 to be selected. Thus, the number of different possible hands is $_{52}C_5 = \frac{52!}{5! \times 47!} = 2{,}598{,}960$.

COMPLEMENT OF AN EVENT

Sometimes it may be easier to calculate the possibility of something not happening, or the complement of an event. Represented by the symbol $\bar{A}$, the complement of A is the probability that event A does not happen. When you know the probability of event A occurring, you can use the formula $P(\bar{A}) = 1 - P(A)$, where $P(\bar{A})$ is the probability of event A not occurring, and $P(A)$ is the probability of event A occurring.

ADDITION RULE

The addition rule for probability is used for finding the probability of a compound event. Use the formula $P(A \text{ or } B) = P(A) + P(B) - P(A \text{ and } B)$, where $P(A)$ is the probability of the event A occurring, $P(B)$ is the probability of event B occurring, and $P(A \text{ and } B)$ is the probability of both events occurring to find the probability of a compound event. The probability of both events occurring at the same time must be subtracted to eliminate any overlap in the first two probabilities.

CONDITIONAL PROBABILITY

Conditional probability is the probability of a dependent event occurring once the original event has already occurred. Given event A and dependent event B, the probability of event B occurring when event A has already occurred is represented by the notation $P(A|B)$. To find the probability of event B occurring, take into account the fact that event A has already occurred and adjust the total number of possible outcomes. For example, suppose you have ten balls numbered 1–10 and you want ball number 7 to be drawn in two draws. On the first draw, the probability of getting the 7 is $\frac{1}{10}$ because there is one ball with a 7 on it and 10 balls to choose from. Assuming the first draw did not yield a 7, the probability of drawing a 7 on the second draw is now $\frac{1}{9}$ because there are only 9 balls remaining for the second draw.

MULTIPLICATION RULE

The multiplication rule can be used to find the probability of two independent events occurring using the formula $P(A \text{ and } B) = P(A) P(B)$, where $P(A \text{ and } B)$ is the probability of two independent events occurring, $P(A)$ is the probability of the first event occurring, and $P(B)$ is the probability of the second event occurring.

The multiplication rule can also be used to find the probability of two dependent events occurring using the formula $P(A \text{ and } B) = P(A) \cdot P(B|A)$, where $P(A \text{ and } B)$ is the probability of two dependent events occurring, $P(A)$ is the probability of the first event occurring, and $P(B|A)$ is the probability of the second event occurring after the first event has already occurred.

Use a **combination of the multiplication** rule and the rule of complements to find the probability that at least one outcome of the element will occur. This is given by the general formula $P(\text{at least one event occurring}) = 1 - P(\text{no outcomes occurring})$. For example, to find the probability that at least one even number will show when a pair of dice is rolled, find the probability that two odd numbers will be rolled (no even numbers) and subtract from one. You can always use a tree diagram or make a chart to list the possible outcomes when the sample space is small, such as in the dice-rolling example, but in most cases it will be much faster to use the multiplication and complement formulas.

> **Review Video: Multiplication Rule**
> Visit mometrix.com/academy and enter code: 782598

EXPECTED VALUE

Expected value is a method of determining the expected outcome in a random situation. It is really a sum of the weighted probabilities of the possible outcomes. Multiply the probability of an event occurring by the weight assigned to that probability (such as the amount of money won or lost). A practical application of the expected value is to determine whether a game of chance is really fair. If the sum of the weighted probabilities is equal to zero, the game is generally considered fair because the player has a fair chance to at least to break even. If the expected value is less than zero, then players lose more than they win. For example, a lottery drawing might allow the player to choose any three-digit number, 000–999. The probability of choosing the winning number is 1:1,000. If it costs \$1 to play, and a winning number receives \$500, the expected value is $\left(-\$1 \cdot \frac{999}{1,000}\right) + \left(\$500 \cdot \frac{1}{1,000}\right) = -0.499$ or $-\$0.50$. In other words, you can expect to lose, on average, 50 cents for every dollar you spend.

EXPERIMENTAL PROBABILITY

Most of the time, when we talk about probability, we mean theoretical probability. Experimental probability, or empirical probability or relative frequency, is the number of times an outcome occurs in a particular experiment or a certain number of observed events. While theoretical

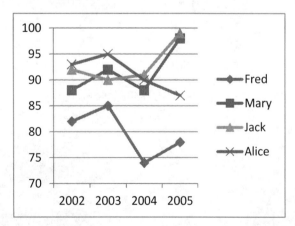

probability is based on what *should* happen, experimental probability is based on what *has* happened. Experimental probability is calculated in the same way as theoretical, except that actual outcomes are used instead of possible outcomes.

Theoretical and experimental probability do not always line up with one another. Theoretical probability says that out of 20 coin tosses, 10 should be heads. However, if we were actually to toss 20 coins, we might record just 5 heads. This doesn't mean that our theoretical probability is incorrect; it just means that this particular experiment had different results from what was predicted. A practical application of empirical probability is the insurance industry. There are no set functions that define life span, health, or safety. Insurance companies look at factors from hundreds of thousands of individuals to find patterns that they then use to set the formulas for insurance premiums.

OBJECTIVE PROBABILITY

Objective probability is based on mathematical formulas and documented evidence. Examples of objective probability include raffles or lottery drawings with a predetermined number of possible outcomes and a predetermined number of outcomes that correspond to an event. Other cases of objective probability include probabilities of rolling dice, flipping coins, or drawing cards. Most gambling games are based on objective probability.

SUBJECTIVE PROBABILITY

Subjective probability is based on personal or professional feelings and judgments. Often, there is a lot of guesswork following extensive research. Areas where subjective probability is applicable include sales trends and business expenses. Attractions set admission prices based on subjective probabilities of attendance, based on varying admission rates, in an effort to maximize their profit.

COMMON CHARTS AND GRAPHS

BAR GRAPH, LINE GRAPH, AND PICTOGRAPH

A bar graph uses bars to compare data, as if each bar were a ruler being used to measure the data. The graph includes a scale that identifies the units being measured. A line graph connects points to show how data increases or decreases over time. The time line is the horizontal axis. The connecting lines between data points on the graph are a way to more clearly show how the data changes. The image below is a line graph.

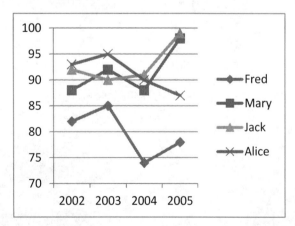

A pictograph uses pictures or symbols to show data. The pictograph has a key to identify what each symbol represents. Generally, each symbol stands for one or more objects.

PIE CHART

A pie chart or circle graph is a diagram used to compare parts of a whole. The full pie represents the whole, and it is divided into sectors that each represent a part of the whole. Each sector or slice of the pie is either labeled to indicate what it represents, or explained on a key associated with the chart. The size of each slice is determined by its percentage of the whole. Numerically, the angle measurement of each sector can be computed by solving the proportion: x/360 = part/whole.

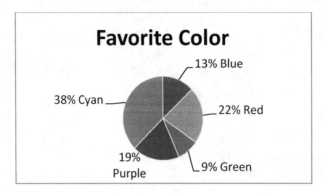

HISTOGRAM

A histogram is a special type of bar graph where the data are grouped in intervals (for example 20–29, 30–39, 40–49, etc.). The frequency, or number of times a value occurs in each interval, is indicated by the height of the bar. The intervals do not have to be the same amount but usually are (all data in ranges of 10 or all in ranges of 5, for example). The smaller the intervals, the more detailed the information.

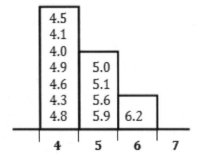

STEM-AND-LEAF PLOT

A stem-and-leaf plot is a way to organize data visually so that the information is easy to understand. A stem-and-leaf plot is simple to construct because a simple line separates the stem (the part of the plot listing the tens digit, if displaying two-digit data) from the leaf (the part that shows the ones digit). Thus, the number 45 would appear as 4 | 5. The stem-and-leaf plot for test scores of a group of 11 students might look like the following:

```
9 | 5
8 | 1, 3, 8
7 | 0, 2, 4, 6, 7
6 | 2, 8
```

A stem-and-leaf plot is similar to a histogram or other frequency plot, but with a stem-and-leaf plot, all the original data is preserved. In this example, while all data has been maintained, it can be seen at a glance that nearly half the students scored in the 70's. These plots can be used for larger numbers as well, but they tend to work better for small sets of data as they can become unwieldy with larger sets.

EQUATIONS AND GRAPHING

When algebraic functions and equations are shown graphically, they are usually shown on a Cartesian Coordinate Plane. This consists of two number lines placed perpendicular to each other and intersecting at the zero point, also known as the origin. The horizontal number line is known as the x-axis, with positive values to the right of the origin and negative values to the left of the origin. The vertical number line is known as the y-axis, with positive values above the origin and negative values below the origin. Any point on the plane can be identified by an ordered pair in the form (x,y), called coordinates. The x-value of the coordinate is called the abscissa, and the y-value of the coordinate is called the ordinate. The two number lines divide the plane into four quadrants: I, II, III, and IV.

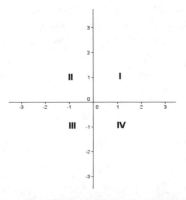

Review Video: Cartesian Coordinate Plane and Graphing
Visit mometrix.com/academy and enter code: 115173

Before learning the different forms of equations, it is important to understand some terminology. A ratio of the change in the vertical distance to the change in horizontal distance is called the slope. On a graph with two points, (x_1, y_1) and (x_2, y_2), the slope is represented by the formula $m = \frac{y_2-y_1}{x_2-x_1}$; $x_1 \neq x_2$. If the value of the slope is positive, the line slopes upward from left to right. If the value of the slope is negative, the line slopes downward from left to right. If the y-coordinates are the same for both points, the slope is 0 and the line is horizontal. If the x-coordinates are the same for both points, there is no slope and the line is vertical. Two or more lines with equal slopes are parallel. Perpendicular lines have slopes that are negative reciprocals of each other, such as $\frac{a}{b}$ and $\frac{-b}{a}$.

Equations are made up of monomials and polynomials. A monomial is a single variable or product of constants and variables, such as x, $2x$, or $\frac{2}{x}$. There will never be addition or subtraction symbols in a monomial. Like monomials have like variables, but they may have different coefficients. Polynomials are algebraic expressions that use addition and subtraction to combine two or more monomials. Two terms make a binomial, three terms make a trinomial, etc. The degree of a monomial is the sum of the exponents of the variables. The degree of a polynomial is the highest degree of any individual term.

As mentioned previously, equations can be written many ways. Below is a list of the many forms equations can take.

- Standard Form: $Ax + By = C$; the slope is $\frac{-A}{B}$ and the y-intercept is $\frac{C}{B}$.
- Slope Intercept Form: $y = mx + b$, where m is the slope and b is the y-intercept.
- Point-Slope Form: $y - y_1 = m(x - x_1)$, where m is the slope and (x_1, y_1) is a point on the line.
- Two-Point Form: $\frac{y-y_1}{x-x_1} = \frac{y_2-y_1}{x_2-x_1}$, where (x_1, y_1) and (x_2, y_2) are two points on the given line.
- Intercept Form: $\frac{x}{x_1} + \frac{y}{y_1} = 1$, where $(x_1, 0)$ is the point at which a line intersects the x-axis, and $(0, y_1)$ is the point at which the same line intersects the y-axis.

Equations can also be written as $ax + b = 0$, where $a \neq 0$. These are referred to as One Variable Linear Equations. A solution to such an equation is called a root. For example, in the equation $5x + 10 = 0$, if we solve for x we get a solution of $x = -2$. In other words, the root of the equation is –2. This is found by first subtracting 10 from both sides, which gives $5x = -10$. Next, simply divide both sides by the coefficient of the variable, in this case 5, to get $x = -2$. This can be checked by plugging –2 back into the original equation $(5)(-2) + 10 = -10 + 10 = 0$.

Geometry

LINES AND PLANES
POINT, LINE, AND PLANE

A point is a fixed location in space with no size or dimensions. It is commonly represented by a A **point** is a fixed location in space, has no size or dimensions, and is commonly represented by a dot. A **line** is a set of points that extends infinitely in two opposite directions. It has length, but no width or depth. A line can be defined by any two distinct points that it contains. A **line segment** is a portion of a line that has definite endpoints. A **ray** is a portion of a line that extends from a single point on that line in one direction along the line. It has a definite beginning, but no ending. A plane is a two-dimensional flat surface defined by three noncollinear points. A plane extends an infinite distance in all directions in those two dimensions. It contains an infinite number of points, parallel lines and segments, intersecting lines and segments, as well as parallel or intersecting rays. A plane will never contain a three-dimensional figure or skew lines. Two given planes will either be parallel or will intersect to form a line. A plane may intersect a circular conic surface such as a cone to form conic sections such as the parabola, hyperbola, circle, or ellipse.

PERPENDICULAR LINES, PARALLEL LINES, AND BISECTORS

Perpendicular lines intersect each other at right angles. They are represented by the symbol ⊥. The shortest distance from a line to a point not on the line is a perpendicular segment from the point to the line. Parallel lines lie in the same plane. They have no points in common and never meet. It is possible for lines to be in different planes, have no points in common, and never meet, but not be parallel because they are in different planes. A bisector is a line or segment that divides another segment into two equal lengths. A perpendicular bisector of a line segment is composed of points that are equidistant from the endpoints of the segment it is dividing.

INTERSECTING LINES, CONCURRENT LINES, AND TRANSVERSALS

Intersecting lines have exactly one point in common. Concurrent lines are multiple lines that intersect at a single point. A transversal is a line that intersects at least two other lines, which may or may not be parallel to one another. A transversal that intersects parallel lines is a common occurrence in geometry.

ANGLES

An angle is formed when two lines or line segments meet at a common point. It may be a common starting point for a pair of segments or rays, or it may be the intersection of lines. Angles are represented by the symbol ∠. The vertex is the point at which two segments or rays meet to form an angle. If the angle is formed by intersecting rays, lines, and/or line segments, the vertex is the point at which four angles are formed. The pairs of angles opposite one another are called vertical angles, and their measures are equal.

There are various types of angles:

- An acute angle has a degree measure less than 90°.
- A right angle has a degree measure of exactly 90°.
- An obtuse angle has a degree measure greater than 90° but less than 180°.
- A straight angle has a degree measure of exactly 180°. This is also a semicircle.
- A reflex angle has a degree measure greater than 180° but less than 360°.
- A full angle has a degree measure of exactly 360°.

Two angles whose sum is exactly 90° are said to be complementary angles. The two angles may or may not be adjacent. In a right triangle, the two acute angles are complementary. Two angles whose sum is exactly 180° are said to be supplementary angles. The two angles may or may not be adjacent. Two intersecting lines always form two pairs of supplementary angles. Adjacent supplementary angles will always form a straight line. Two angles that have the same vertex and share a side are said to be adjacent. Vertical angles are not adjacent because they share a vertex but no common side.

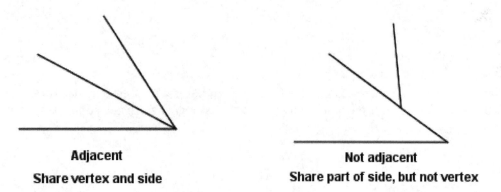

Adjacent
Share vertex and side

Not adjacent
Share part of side, but not vertex

When two parallel lines are cut by a transversal, the angles between the two parallel lines are interior angles and the angles that are outside the parallel lines are exterior angles. In the diagram below, angles 3, 4, 5, and 6 are interior angles. Angles 1, 2, 7, and 8 are exterior angles.

When two parallel lines are cut by a transversal, the angles that are in the same position relative to the transversal and a parallel line are corresponding angles. The diagram below has four pairs of corresponding angles: angles 1 and 5, angles 2 and 6, angles 3 and 7, and angles 4 and 8. Corresponding angles formed by parallel lines are congruent.

When two parallel lines are cut by a transversal, the two interior angles on opposite sides of the transversal are called alternate interior angles. In the diagram below, there are two pairs of alternate interior angles: angles 3 and 6, and angles 4 and 5. Alternate interior angles formed by parallel lines are congruent. When two parallel lines are cut by a transversal, the two exterior angles that are on opposite sides of the transversal are called alternate exterior angles. In the diagram below, there are two pairs of alternate exterior angles: angles 1 and 8, and angles 2 and 7. Alternate exterior angles formed by parallel lines are congruent. Congruent angles are represented by the symbol ≅.

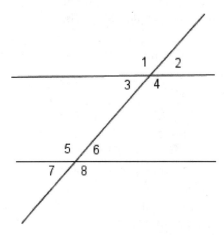

When two lines intersect, four angles are formed. The nonadjacent angles at this vertex are called vertical angles. Vertical angles are congruent. In the diagram, $\angle ABD \cong \angle CBE$ and $\angle ABC \cong \angle DBE$.

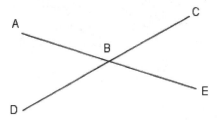

TRIANGLES

An equilateral triangle has three congruent sides. An equilateral triangle also has three congruent angles, 60° each. All equilateral triangles are also acute triangles since each angle is less than 90°.

An isosceles triangle has two congruent sides. An isosceles triangle also has two congruent angles opposite the two congruent sides.

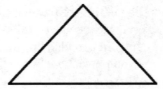

A scalene triangle has no congruent sides. A scalene triangle also has three angles of different measures. The angle with the largest measure is opposite the longest side, and the angle with the smallest measure is opposite the shortest side.

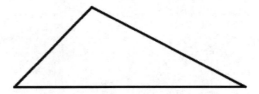

An acute triangle is a triangle with all three angles less than 90°. If two of the angles are equal, the acute triangle is also an isosceles triangle. If the three angles are all equal, the acute triangle is also an equilateral triangle.

A right triangle has exactly one angle equal to 90°. All right triangles follow the Pythagorean Theorem ($a^2 + b^2 = c^2$). A right triangle can never be acute or obtuse.

An obtuse triangle has exactly one angle greater than 90°. The other two angles may or may not be equal. If the two remaining angles are equal, the obtuse triangle is also an isosceles triangle.

TRIANGLE TERMINOLOGY

- Altitude—a line segment drawn from one vertex perpendicular to the opposite side. In the diagram below, $\overline{BE}$, $\overline{AD}$, and $\overline{CF}$ are altitudes. The three altitudes in a triangle are always concurrent.

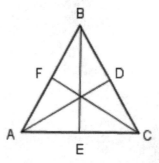

- Height—the length of the altitude, although the two terms are often used interchangeably.
- Orthocenter—the point of concurrency of the altitudes of a triangle. Note that in an obtuse triangle, the orthocenter will be outside the triangle, and in a right triangle, the orthocenter is the vertex of the right angle.

- Median—a line segment drawn from one vertex to the midpoint of the opposite side. This is not necessarily the same as the altitude, except the altitude to the base of an isosceles triangle and all three altitudes of an equilateral triangle.
- Centroid—the point of concurrency of the medians of a triangle. Only in an equilateral triangle is this the same point as the orthocenter. Unlike the orthocenter, the centroid is always inside the triangle. The centroid can also be considered the exact center of the triangle. Any shape of triangle can be perfectly balanced on a tip placed at the centroid. The centroid is also two-thirds of the distance from the vertex to the opposite side.

PYTHAGOREAN THEOREM

In a right triangle, the side opposite the right angle is called the hypotenuse. The other two sides are called the legs. The Pythagorean Theorem states the relationship between the legs and hypotenuse of a right triangle: $a^2 + b^2 = c^2$, where a and b are the lengths of the legs and c is the length of the hypotenuse. Note that this formula will only work with right triangles.

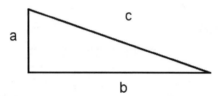

GENERAL RULES

The Triangle Inequality Theorem states that the sum of the measures of any two sides of a triangle is always greater than the measure of the third side. If the sum of the measures of two sides were equal to the third side, a triangle would be impossible because the two sides would lie flat across the third side and there would be no vertex. If the sum of the measures of two of the sides was less than the third side, a closed figure would be impossible because the two shortest sides would never meet.

The sum of the measures of the interior angles of a triangle is always 180°. Therefore, a triangle can never have more than one angle greater than or equal to 90°.

In any triangle, the angles opposite congruent sides are congruent, and the sides opposite congruent angles are congruent. The largest angle is always opposite the longest side, and the smallest angle is always opposite the shortest side.

The line segment that joins the midpoints of any two sides of a triangle is always parallel to the third side and exactly half the length of the third side.

SIMILARITY AND CONGRUENCE RULES

Similar triangles are triangles whose corresponding angles are equal and whose corresponding sides are proportional. Represented by AAA. Similar triangles whose corresponding sides are congruent are also congruent triangles.

Triangles can be shown to be **congruent** in 5 ways:

- **SSS**: Three sides of one triangle are congruent to the three corresponding sides of the second triangle.
- **SAS**: Two sides and the included angle (the angle formed by those two sides) of one triangle are congruent to the corresponding two sides and included angle of the second triangle.

- **ASA**: Two angles and the included side (the side that joins the two angles) of one triangle are congruent to the corresponding two angles and included side of the second triangle.
- **AAS**: Two angles and a non-included side of one triangle are congruent to the corresponding two angles and non-included side of the second triangle.
- **HL**: The hypotenuse and leg of one right triangle are congruent to the corresponding hypotenuse and leg of the second right triangle.

> **Review Video: Similar Triangles**
> Visit mometrix.com/academy and enter code: 398538
>
> **Review Video: What is a Congruent Shape?**
> Visit mometrix.com/academy and enter code: 492281

AREA AND PERIMETER FORMULAS

The perimeter of any triangle is found by summing the three side lengths: $P = a + b + c$. For an equilateral triangle, this is the same as $P = 3s$, where s is any side length, since all three sides are the same length.

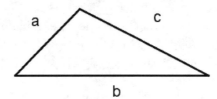

The area of any triangle can be found by taking half the product of one side length (base or b) and the perpendicular distance from that side to the opposite vertex (height or h). In equation form, $A = \frac{1}{2}bh$. For many triangles, it may be difficult to calculate h, so using one of the other formulas given here may be easier.

Another formula that works for any triangle is $A = \sqrt{s(s-a)(s-b)(s-c)}$, where A is the area, s is the semiperimeter $s = \frac{a+b+c}{2}$, and a, b, and c are the lengths of the three sides.

The area of an equilateral triangle can found by the formula $A = \frac{\sqrt{3}}{4}s^2$, where A is the area and s is the length of a side. You could also use the 30° - 60° - 90° ratios to find the height of the triangle and then use the standard triangle area formula, but this is faster.

The area of an isosceles triangle can found by the formula $A = \frac{1}{2}b\sqrt{a^2 - \frac{b^2}{4}}$, where A is the area, b is the base (the unique side), and a is the length of one of the two congruent sides. If you do not

139

remember this formula, you can use the Pythagorean Theorem to find the height so you can use the standard formula for the area of a triangle.

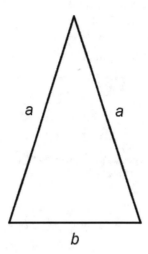

POLYGONS

Each straight line segment of a polygon is called a side. The point at which two sides of a polygon intersect is called the vertex. In a polygon, the number of sides is always equal to the number of vertices. A polygon with all sides congruent and all angles equal is called a regular polygon. A line segment from the center of a polygon, perpendicular to a side of the polygon, is called the apothem. In a regular polygon, the apothem can be used to find the area of the polygon using the formula $A = \frac{1}{2}ap$, where a is the apothem and p is the perimeter. A line segment from the center of a polygon to a vertex of the polygon is called a radius. The radius of a regular polygon is also the radius of a circle that can be circumscribed about the polygon.

- Triangle—3-sided polygon
- Quadrilateral—4-sided polygon
- Pentagon—5-sided polygon
- Hexagon—6-sided polygon
- Heptagon—7-sided polygon
- Octagon—8-sided polygon
- Nonagon—9-sided polygon
- Decagon—10-sided polygon
- Dodecagon—12-sided polygon

More generally, an n-gon is a polygon that has n angles and n sides.

The sum of the interior angles of an n-sided polygon is $(n-2) \times 180°$. For example, in a triangle $n = 3$. So the sum of the interior angles is $(3-2) \times 180° = 180°$. In a quadrilateral, $n = 4$, and the sum of the angles is $(4-2) \times 180° = 360°$.

A diagonal is a line segment that joins two nonadjacent vertices of a polygon.

A convex polygon is a polygon whose diagonals all lie within the interior of the polygon.

140

A concave polygon has at least one diagonal that lies outside the polygon. In the diagram below, quadrilateral *ABCD* is concave because diagonal $\overline{AC}$ lies outside the polygon.

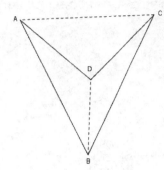

The number of diagonals in a polygon can be found by using the formula: $\frac{n(n-3)}{2}$, where *n* is the number of sides in the polygon. This formula works for all polygons, not just regular polygons.

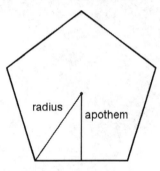

Congruent figures are geometric figures that have the same size and shape. All corresponding angles are equal, and all corresponding sides are equal. Congruence is indicated by the symbol ≅.

Congruent polygons

Similar figures are geometric figures that have the same shape, but do not necessarily have the same size. All corresponding angles are equal, and all corresponding sides are proportional, but they do not have to be equal. Similar figures are indicated by the symbol ~.

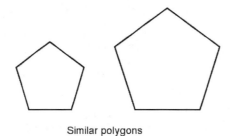

Similar polygons

Note that all congruent figures are also similar, but not all similar figures are congruent.

A line of symmetry divides a figure or object into two symmetric parts. Each symmetric half is congruent to the other. An object may have no lines of symmetry, one line of symmetry, or more than one line of symmetry.

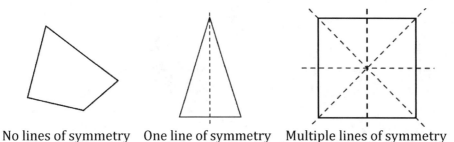

No lines of symmetry   One line of symmetry   Multiple lines of symmetry

> **Review Video: <u>Polygons</u>**
> Visit mometrix.com/academy and enter code: 271869

QUADRILATERALS

A quadrilateral is a closed, two-dimensional geometric figure composed of exactly four straight sides. The sum of the interior angles of any quadrilateral is 360°. A quadrilateral whose diagonals bisect each other is a parallelogram. A quadrilateral whose opposite sides are parallel (2 pairs of parallel sides) is a parallelogram. A quadrilateral whose diagonals are perpendicular bisectors of each other is a rhombus. A quadrilateral whose opposite sides (both pairs) are parallel and congruent is a rhombus. A parallelogram with right angles is a rectangle. A rhombus with right angles is a square. Because the rhombus is a form of parallelogram, the rules about the angles of a parallelogram also apply to the rhombus.

PARALLELOGRAM

A parallelogram is a quadrilateral with exactly two pairs of opposite parallel sides. The parallel sides are also congruent. The opposite interior angles are always congruent, and the consecutive interior angles are supplementary. The diagonals of a parallelogram bisect each other. Each diagonal divides the parallelogram into two congruent triangles.

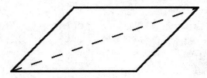

TRAPEZOID

Traditionally, a trapezoid is a quadrilateral that has exactly one pair of parallel sides. Some math texts define a trapezoid as a quadrilateral with at least one pair of parallel sides. Because there are no rules governing the second pair of sides, there are no rules that apply to the properties of the diagonals of a trapezoid.

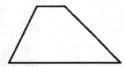

RECTANGLES, RHOMBUSES, AND SQUARES

Rectangles, rhombuses, and squares are all special forms of parallelograms. A rectangle is a parallelogram with right angles. All rectangles are parallelograms, but not all parallelograms are rectangles. The diagonals of a rectangle are congruent.

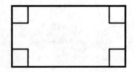

A rhombus is a parallelogram with four congruent sides. All rhombuses are parallelograms, but not all parallelograms are rhombuses. The diagonals of a rhombus are perpendicular to each other.

A square is a parallelogram with four right angles and four congruent sides. All squares are also parallelograms, rhombuses, and rectangles. The diagonals of a square are congruent and perpendicular to each other.

AREA AND PERIMETER FORMULAS

The area of a square is found by using the formula $A = s^2$, where s is the length of one side.

143

The perimeter of a square is found by using the formula $P = 4s$, where s is the length of one side.

The area of a rectangle is found by the formula $A = lw$, where A is the area of the rectangle, l is the length (usually considered to be the longer side), and w is the width (usually considered to be the shorter side). The numbers for l and w are interchangeable.

The perimeter of a rectangle is found by the formula $P = 2l + 2w$ or $P = 2(l + w)$, where l is the length and w is the width. It may be easier to add the length and width first and then double the result, as in the second formula.

The area of a parallelogram is found by the formula $A = bh$, where b is the length of the base and h is the height. Note that the base and height correspond to the length and width in a rectangle, so this formula would apply to rectangles as well. Do not confuse the height of a parallelogram with the length of the second side. The two are only the same measure in the case of a rectangle.

The perimeter of a parallelogram is found by the formula $P = 2a + 2b$ or $P = 2(a + b)$, where a and b are the lengths of the two sides.

The area of a trapezoid is found by the formula $A = \frac{1}{2}h(b_1 + b_2)$, where h is the height (segment joining and perpendicular to the parallel bases), and b_1 and b_2 are the two parallel sides (bases). Do not use one of the other two sides as the height unless that side is also perpendicular to the parallel bases.

The perimeter of a trapezoid is found by the formula $P = a + b_1 + c + b_2$, where a, b_1, c, and b_2 are the four sides of the trapezoid.

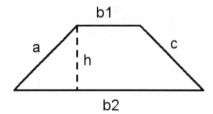

CIRCLES

The center is the single point inside the circle that is equidistant from every point on the circle (Point O in the diagram below.) The radius is a line segment that joins the center of the circle and any one point on the circle. All radii of a circle are equal (Segments OX, OY, and OZ in the diagram below.) The diameter is a line segment that passes through the center of the circle and has both endpoints on the circle. The diameter is exactly twice the length of the radius (Segment XZ in the diagram below.)

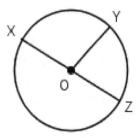

The area of a circle is found by the formula $A = \pi r^2$, where r is the radius. If the diameter is given, remember to divide it in half to get the length of the radius before proceeding. The circumference of a circle is found by the formula $C = 2\pi r$, where r is the radius. Again, remember to convert the diameter if you are given that measure rather than the radius.

Concentric circles have the same center, but not the same length of radii. A bull's-eye target is an example of concentric circles (one inside the other).

An arc is a portion of a circle. Specifically, an arc is the set of points between and including two points on a circle. An arc does not contain any points inside the circle. When a segment is drawn from the endpoints of an arc to the center of the circle, a sector is formed.

A central angle is an angle whose vertex is the center of a circle and whose legs intercept an arc of the circle. Angle *XOY* in the diagram above is a central angle. A minor arc is an arc that has a measure less than 180°. The measure of a central angle is equal to the measure of the minor arc it intercepts. A major arc has a measure of at least 180°. The measure of the major arc can be found by subtracting the measure of the central angle from 360°.

A semicircle is an arc whose endpoints are the endpoints of the diameter of a circle. A semicircle is exactly half of a circle.

An inscribed angle is an angle whose vertex lies on a circle and whose legs contain chords of that circle. The portion of the circle intercepted by the legs of the angle is called the intercepted arc. The measure of the intercepted arc is exactly twice the measure of the inscribed angle. In the diagram below, angle *ABC* is an inscribed angle. $\overset{\frown}{AC} = 2(m\angle ABC)$

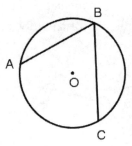

Any angle inscribed in a semicircle is a right angle. The intercepted arc is 180°, making the inscribed angle half that, or 90°. In the diagram below, angle *ABC* is inscribed in semicircle *ABC*, making angle *ABC* equal to 90°.

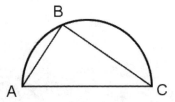

A chord is a line segment that has both endpoints on a circle. In the diagram below, $\overline{EB}$ is a chord.

A secant is a line that passes through a circle and contains a chord of that circle. In the diagram below, $\overleftrightarrow{EB}$ is a secant and contains chord $\overline{EB}$.

A tangent is a line in the same plane as a circle, touching the circle at exactly one point. While a line segment can be tangent to a circle as part of a line that is tangent, it is improper to say a tangent can simply be a line segment that touches the circle in exactly one point. In the diagram below, $\overleftrightarrow{CD}$ is tangent to circle A. Notice that $\overline{FB}$ is not tangent to the circle. $\overline{FB}$ is a line segment that touches the circle at exactly one point, but if the segment were extended, it would touch the circle at a second point. The point at which a tangent touches a circle is called the point of tangency. In the diagram below, point B is the point of tangency.

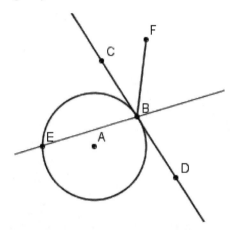

A secant is a line that intersects a circle at two points. Two secants may intersect inside the circle, on the circle, or outside the circle. When the two secants intersect on the circle, an inscribed angle is formed.

When two secants intersect inside a circle, the measure of each of two vertical angles is equal to half the sum of the two intercepted arcs. In the diagram below, $m\angle AEB = \frac{1}{2}(\widehat{AB} + \widehat{CD})$ and $m\angle BEC = \frac{1}{2}(\widehat{BC} + \widehat{AD})$.

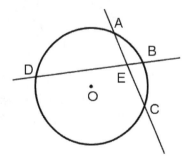

When two secants intersect outside a circle, the measure of the angle formed is equal to half the difference of the two arcs that lie between the two secants. In the diagram below, $m\angle E = \frac{1}{2}(\widehat{AB} - \widehat{CD})$.

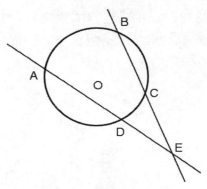

The arc length is the length of the portion of the circumference between two points on the circle. The formula for arc length is $s = \frac{\pi r \theta}{180°}$ where s is the arc length, r is the length of the radius, and θ is the angular measure of the arc in degrees, or $s = r\theta$, where θ is the angular measure of the arc in radians (2π radians = 360 degrees).

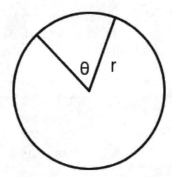

A sector is the portion of a circle formed by two radii and their intercepted arc. While the arc length is defined exclusively as the points that are also on the circumference of the circle, the sector is the entire area bounded by the arc and the two radii.

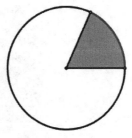

The area of a sector of a circle is found by the formula $A = \frac{\theta r^2}{2}$, where A is the area, θ is the measure of the central angle in radians, and r is the radius. To find the area when the central angle is in degrees, use the formula $A = \frac{\theta \pi r^2}{360}$, where θ is the measure of the central angle in degrees and r is the radius.

A circle is inscribed in a polygon if each of the sides of the polygon is tangent to the circle. A polygon is inscribed in a circle if each of the vertices of the polygon lies on the circle.

A circle is circumscribed about a polygon if each of the vertices of the polygon lies on the circle. A polygon is circumscribed about the circle if each of the sides of the polygon is tangent to the circle.

If one figure is inscribed in another, then the other figure is circumscribed about the first figure.

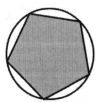

Circle circumscribed about a pentagon

Pentagon inscribed in a circle

SOLIDS
AREA

The surface area of a solid object is the area of all sides or exterior surfaces. For objects such as prisms and pyramids, a further distinction is made between base surface area (B) and lateral surface area (LA). For a prism, the total surface area (SA) is $SA = LA + 2B$. For a pyramid or cone, the total surface area is $SA = LA + B$.

The surface area of a sphere can be found by the formula $A = 4\pi r^2$, where r is the radius.

VOLUME

The volume of a sphere is given by the formula $V = \frac{4}{3}\pi r^3$, where r is the radius. Both volume and surface area are generally given in terms of π.

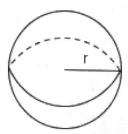

The volume of any prism is found by the formula $V = Bh$, where B is the area of the base and h is the height (perpendicular distance between the bases). The surface area of any prism is the sum of the areas of both bases and all sides. It can be calculated as $SA = 2B + Ph$, where P is the perimeter of the base.

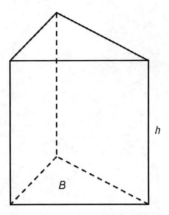

The volume of a rectangular prism can be found by the formula $V = lwh$, where V is the volume, l is the length, w is the width, and h is the height. The surface area of a rectangular prism can be calculated as $SA = 2lw + 2hl + 2wh$ or $SA = 2(lw + hl + wh)$.

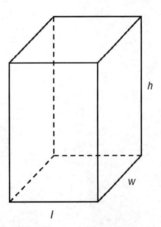

> **Review Video: Volume and Surface Area of a Prism**
> Visit mometrix.com/academy and enter code: 420158

The volume of a cube can be found by the formula $V = s^3$, where s is the length of a side. The surface area of a cube is calculated as $SA = 6s^2$, where SA is the total surface area and s is the length of a side. These formulas are the same as the ones used for the volume and surface area of a rectangular prism, but simplified since all three quantities (length, width, and height) are the same.

The volume of a cylinder can be calculated by the formula $V = \pi r^2 h$, where r is the radius and h is the height. The surface area of a cylinder can be found by the formula $SA = 2\pi r^2 + 2\pi rh$. The first term is the base area multiplied by two, and the second term is the perimeter of the base multiplied by the height.

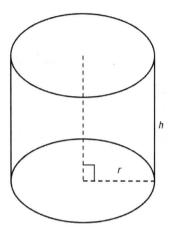

Mathematics Practice Test

1. Which of the following numbers is the greatest?

    a. 10^3
    b. 108.7
    c. $\sqrt{10,000}$
    d. −1025

2. Miguel buys a loaf of bread at the grocery store for $4.25. He also buys two bottles of soda for $2.15 each, a chocolate bar for $1.90, a bottle of shampoo for $5.25, and three magazines for $1.50 each. How much did he spend in all?

    a. $16.05
    b. $19.05
    c. $20.20
    d. $20.45

3. A charity organization is preparing a fund-raising dinner. The goal is to raise $27,000. They must pay costs of $1,000 to rent the hall for the evening, plus $2,500 in wages for staff and $25.00 per plate of food served. If tickets to the dinner cost $150, how many tickets must the organization sell in order to reach their goal?

    a. 180
    b. 216
    c. 244
    d. 281

4. In the right triangle shown below, side AB is twice the length of side BC. What is the area of the triangle in cm²?

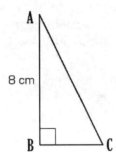

    a. 8
    b. 16
    c. 24
    d. 32

5. Cassandra must average at least 70 on three math tests to get a passing grade. Her scores on the first two tests were 64 and 80. What is the minimum score she must get on the third test to pass?

    a. 70
    b. 74
    c. 72
    d. 66

6. What is the least common denominator for the fractions $\frac{1}{15}, \frac{1}{21}$, and $\frac{1}{14}$?

    a. 5
    b. 210
    c. 140
    d. 91

7. The area of a circle is 8π. What is the length of the radius?

    a. $2\sqrt{2}$
    b. 4
    c. 8
    d. $3\sqrt{2}$

8. An airplane flies from New York to San Francisco, a distance of 2,700 miles, at constant airspeed in 6 ½ hours. The return flight, at the same airspeed, takes 6 hours. Determine the speed of the wind, assuming it to be constant.

    a. 65 mph
    b. 35 mph
    c. 17.5 mph
    d. 15.5 mph

9. Andrea runs 4 miles every day, but she wants to increase her distance in order to run a 26-mile marathon. She decides to add 2 miles each day to her distance until she achieves her goal. If she starts with 6 miles today, how many miles will she have run, in total, by the time she achieves her 26-mile goal?

    a. 156
    b. 162
    c. 170
    d. 176

10. The Quality Mushroom Company sells small mushrooms for $5.95 per pound and large mushrooms for $6.95 per pound. How many pounds of large mushrooms should be mixed with 2 pounds of small ones in order to create a mixture that sells for $6.75 per pound?

    a. 4
    b. 6
    c. 8
    d. 10

11. In the figure below, two circles with radii of length R are tangential to one another. The line segment AB joins their centers. A second line segment, AC, extends from the center of one circle and is tangential to the other. What is the length of the line segment AC?

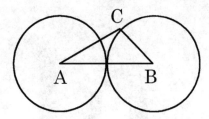

  a. $3R$
  b. $2\sqrt{R}$
  c. $R\sqrt{2}$
  d. $R\sqrt{3}$

12. Which of the following represents an irrational number?

  a. 1.7
  b. $\sqrt{16}$
  c. $\dfrac{1}{4}$
  d. $\sqrt{12}$

13. Identify the median of the following data set: {12, 14, 45, 9, 7, 16, 13, 4}.

  a. 12
  b. 12.5
  c. 13
  d. 13.5

14. The chart below shows the annual number of visitors to the Augusta Planetarium. Which year shows the greatest increase in visitors over the prior year?

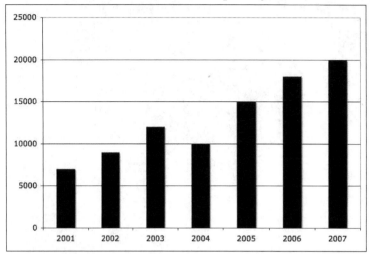

  a. 2002
  b. 2004
  c. 2005
  d. 2007

15. Jenny buys a lottery ticket. It has five digits. For each digit, there is an equal probability that any of the numbers 0 – 9 will be chosen. Jenny's number is 00573. What is the chance that she might win?

  a. $\dfrac{1}{100}$
  b. $\dfrac{1}{1,000}$
  c. $\dfrac{1}{10,000}$
  d. $\dfrac{1}{100,000}$

16. Simplify the expression: $\dfrac{2+\dfrac{4}{y}}{\dfrac{y+2}{3}}$

  a. $\dfrac{y+2}{3}$
  b. $3y$
  c. $\dfrac{6}{y}$
  d. $\dfrac{y-2}{6}$

17. Regina goes to the ice cream store to get a cone with three scoops. There are nine flavors to choose from, and she wants to get three different flavors. How many different combinations of three flavors are possible?

    a. 504
    b. 84
    c. 27
    d. 16

18. The figure below shows two triangles that are _____ .

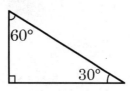

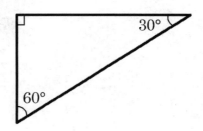

    a. congruent
    b. equilateral
    c. similar
    d. isosceles

19. An automobile manufacturer offers a rebate equivalent to 15% of the list price of a vehicle. If a new sedan normally sells for a list price of $30,000, what is the price that must be paid with the rebate?

    a. $28,500
    b. $27,500
    c. $25,500
    d. $23,500

20. A lumberyard charges $1 per cut to trim boards. Bob buys a 12-ft board and wants it cut into twelve 1-ft pieces. How much will he be charged for the cutting?

    a. $12
    b. $11
    c. $13
    d. $10

21. The sum of 14 and twice a number is 8. What is the number?

   a. 3
   b. −4
   c. −6
   d. −3

22. The figure below shows a circle at center O intersected by a first line that forms a diameter AB and by a second line that forms a chord AC. If the circumference of the circle is 720 m and the angle CAB between the two lines is 20°, what is the length of the arc segment BC?

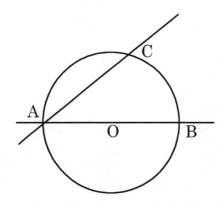

   a. 120 m
   b. 80 m
   c. 75 m
   d. 60 m

23. Find the intersection of the lines represented by the equations $y = -2x + 6$ and $y = 4x + 3$

   a. $(1/2, 5)$
   b. $(2, 5)$
   c. $(2, -3)$
   d. $(3, -2)$

24. If May 7th falls on a Monday, which of the following dates will fall on a Wednesday?

   a. May 21st
   b. May 23rd
   c. May 25th
   d. April 31st

25. Bob and Ken are painting a room. If Bob paints the room alone, he can finish the job in 4 hours. If Ken paints it alone, he can finish the job in 6 hours. How long will it take them to paint it together?

    a. 2 hours
    b. 3 hours 15 minutes
    c. 1 hour 48 minutes
    d. 2 hours 24 minutes

26. In the figure below, a circle with radius r is inscribed within a square. What is the area of the shaded region?

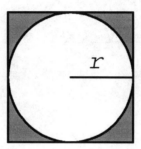

    a. $4r - \pi$
    b. $(4 - \pi)r^2$
    c. $4r^2 - \pi$
    d. $4r - \pi r^2$

27. What is the next term in the sequence 1, 3, 7, 13, 21, ...?

    a. 27
    b. 29
    c. 31
    d. 32

28. Josephine invests a sum of money at 4% interest for a year. At the end of this time, she has earned $200 in interest. What was the original amount of money that she invested?

    a. $5,000
    b. $4,000
    c. $6,000
    d. $6,400

29. A line passes through the points (–1, 2) and (3, 8). What is the slope of the line?

    a. $\dfrac{3}{5}$
    b. $\dfrac{3}{2}$
    c. $\dfrac{-2}{5}$
    d. $\dfrac{6}{5}$

30. An irregular pentagon has three internal right angles and dimensions as shown in the figure below. What is the area in square feet?

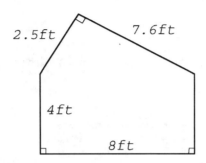

a. 41.5
b. 31.5
c. 46.5
d. 48.6

31. A recipe for making 50 pancakes calls for 24 cups of flour. How many cups of flour are needed to make only 8 pancakes?

a. 3.84
b. 2.95
c. 4.41
d. 4.10

32. The figure below shows a square. If side AD = 10 and if AE = EB and BF = FC, what is the area of the shaded region?

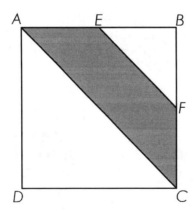

a. 37.5
b. 16.5
c. 24
d. 42.5

33. The sum of three consecutive integers is 36. What is the largest of the three integers?

    a. 17
    b. 14
    c. 13
    d. 12

34. A picture is to be printed onto a sheet of paper with dimensions of 8 ½ x 11 inches. A margin of 1½ inches is to be left on all sides of the picture. What is the area of the printed picture?

    a. 42 in²
    b. 44 in²
    c. 46 in²
    d. 48 in²

35. The figure shows two rectangles. Rectangle I is 50% longer than rectangle II. Rectangle II is 50% wider than rectangle I. What is the ratio of the area of rectangle I to the area of rectangle II?

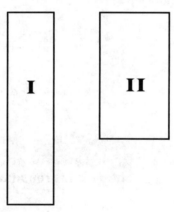

    a. 1:1
    b. 1:2
    c. 1:1.5
    d. 1:1.25

36. If $10x + 2 = 7$, what is the value of $2x$?

    a. 0.5
    b. −0.5
    c. 1
    d. 5
    e. 10

37. A long distance runner does a first lap around a track in exactly 50 seconds. As she tires, each subsequent lap takes 20% longer than the previous one. How long does she take to run 3 laps?

    a. 180 seconds
    b. 182 seconds
    c. 160 seconds
    d. 72 seconds

38. A number *N* is multiplied by 3. The result is the same as when *N* is divided by 3. What is the value of *N*?

    a. 1
    b. 0
    c. −1
    d. 3

39. The letter H exhibits symmetry with respect to a horizontal axis, as shown in the figure, as everything below the dashed line is a mirror image of everything above it. Which of the following letters does NOT exhibit horizontal symmetry?

    a. C
    b. D
    c. E
    d. Z

40. John buys 100 shares of stock at $100 per share. The price goes up by 10% and he sells 50 shares. Then, prices drop by 10% and he sells his remaining 50 shares. How much did he get for the last 50?

    a. $4900
    b. $4950
    c. $5000
    d. $5050

41. The sides of a triangle are equal to integral numbers of units. Two sides are 4 and 6 units long, respectively; what is the minimum value for the triangle's perimeter?

    a. 10 units
    b. 11 units
    c. 12 units
    d. 13 units

42. The two shortest sides of a right triangle are 6 and 8 units long, respectively. What is the length of the perimeter?

    a. 10 units
    b. 18 units
    c. 24 units
    d. 14 units

43. What is the area of an isosceles triangle inscribed in a circle of radius _r_ if the base of the triangle is the diameter of the circle?

    a. r^2

    b. $2r^2$

    c. πr^2

    d. $2\pi r$

44. A regular deck of cards has 52 cards. What is the probability of drawing three aces in a row?

    a. 1 in 52

    b. 1 in 156

    c. 1 in 2,000

    d. 1 in 5,525

45.

Lemons	35%
Sugar	20%
Cups	25%
Stand improvements	5%
Profits	15%

Herbert plans to use the earnings from his lemonade stand according to the table above, for the first month of operations. If he buys $70 worth of lemons, how much profit does he take home?

    a. $15.00

    b. $20.00

    c. $30.00

    d. $35.50

46. A teacher has 3 hours to grade all the papers submitted by the 35 students in her class. She gets through the first 5 papers in 30 minutes. How much faster does she have to work to grade the remaining papers in the allotted time?

    a. 10%

    b. 15%

    c. 20%

    d. 25%

47. A sailor judges the distance to a lighthouse by holding a ruler at arm's length and measuring the apparent height of the lighthouse. He knows that the lighthouse is actually 60 feet tall. If it appears to be 3 inches tall when the ruler is held 2 feet from his eye, how far away is it?

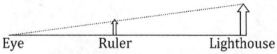

    a. 60 feet

    b. 120 feet

    c. 240 feet

    d. 480 feet

48. Forty students in a class take a test that is graded on a scale of 1 to 10. The histogram in the figure shows the grade distribution, with the *x*-axis representing the grades and the *y*-axis representing the number of students obtaining each grade. If the mean, median, and modal values are represented by *n, p,* and *q*, respectively, which of the following is true?

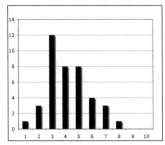

    a. n > p > q
    b. n > q > p
    c. q > p > n
    d. p > q > n

49. Referring to the figure in the previous question, if the top 10% of students are to receive a grade of A, what is the minimum test score that will receive an A?

    a. 10
    b. 9
    c. 8
    d. 7

50. In a game played with toothpicks, players A and B take turns removing toothpicks from a row on a table. At each turn, each player must remove 1, 2, or 3 toothpicks from the row. The object is to force the other player to remove the last toothpick. If there are 6 toothpicks in the row, which of the following moves ensures a win?

    a. Remove 1.
    b. Remove 2.
    c. Remove 3.
    d. There is no way to ensure a win.

51. Which equation is represented by the graph shown below?

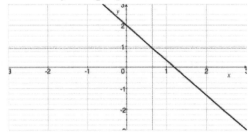

    a. $y = \frac{5}{3}x + 2$
    b. $y = -\frac{5}{3}x - 2$
    c. $y = -\frac{5}{3}x + 2$
    d. $y = \frac{5}{3}x - 2$

52. Determine the volume of a rectangular box with a length of 5 inches, a height of 7 inches, and a width of 9 inches.

    a. 445.095 in³
    b. 315 in³
    c. 45 in³
    d. 35 in³

53. A water sprinkler covers a circular area with a radius of 6 feet. If the water pressure is increased so that the radius increases to 8 feet, by approximately how much is the area covered by the water increased?

    a. 4 square feet
    b. 36 square feet
    c. 64 square feet
    d. 88 square feet

54. The graph below, not drawn to scale, shows a straight line passing through the origin. Point P1 has the (x,y) coordinates (–5,–3). What is the x-coordinate of point P2 if its y-coordinate is 3?

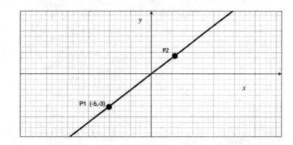

    a. 0.8
    b. 1
    c. 5
    d. 3

55. Equal numbers of dimes and pennies are placed in a single row on a table. Which of the following must be true?

    a. Every dime will be next to a penny.
    b. If there are two dimes at one end of the row, two pennies must be next to one another.
    c. If there is a dime at one end of the row, there must be a penny at the other end.
    d. If there are two pennies together anywhere in the row, there must be dimes at both ends.

56. For the number set {7, 12, 5, 16, 23, 44, 18, 9, Z}, which of the following values could be equal to Z if Z is the median of the set?

    a. 14
    b. 11
    c. 12
    d. 17

57. If Q is divisible by 2 and 7, which of the following is also divisible by 2 and 7?
    a. $Q + 2$
    b. $Q + 7$
    c. $Q + 28$
    d. $Q + 9$

Mathematics Answer Key and Explanations

1. A: In scientific notation, this is 10 raised to the 3rd power, or 1,000. Choice C, the square root of 10,000, equals 100. While the absolute value of Choice D is 1,025, it is a negative number, so that it is not as great as Choice A.

2. C: Add the numbers together, noting that there are two sodas and three magazines: $4.25 + 2($2.15) + $1.90 + $5.25 + 3($1.50) = $4.25 + $4.30 + $1.90 + $5.25 + $4.50 = $20.20.

3. C: Translate the problem into an algebraic equation, and let x equal the number of tickets sold and therefore the number of plates of food that must be purchased. The profit will equal the revenues per plate, minus the cost per plate and the fixed costs of the hall and staff: $27,000 = 150x - 25x - 1000 - 2500$. Simplify: $27,000 = x(150 - 25) - 3500$. Solving for x yields: $x = \frac{30,500}{125} = 244$.

4. B: Note that the area of the triangle is one half the base times the height. Since AB is twice the length of BC, BC = 4 cm and the formula yields $A = \frac{1}{2}(8)(4) = 16$.

5. D: To calculate the average grade, divide the sum of all the grades by the number of tests. This number must equal at least 70. That is, $\frac{Sum}{3} \geq 70$. Solving for the sum shows $Sum \geq 3(70)$, or 210. Since the first two scores, 64 and 80, add up to 144, the third score must be greater or equal to 210–144, or 66.

6. B: The least common denominator, or LCD, is equal to the least common multiple (LCM) of the denominators. To find this, factor the denominators completely: 15 = 3 x 5; 21 = 3 x 7; 14 = 2 x 7. The unique factors are 2, 3, 5, and 7. The product 2 x 3 x 5 x 7 = 210 is therefore the LCD.

7. A: The area of a circle is given by the formula $A = \pi r^2$, where r is the radius. Since $8\pi = \pi r^2$, it follows that $r^2 = 8$ and that $r = \sqrt{8}$. Since 8 = 2 x 4, and $\sqrt{4} = 2$, it follows that $r = 2\sqrt{2}$.

8. C: Solve for both the wind speed w and the speed of the aircraft s by setting up a system of equations. On the eastward leg the wind accelerates the aircraft, so $\frac{2,700}{6} = s + w = 450$. Conversely, on the westward leg, $\frac{2,700}{6.5} = s - w = 415$ (approximately). Subtracting the second equation from the first yields $2w = 35$, so $w = 17.5$ mph.

9. D: Determine the average distance run per day. If Andrea runs 6 miles on day 1 and adds two miles per day, she will reach her goal on day 11, since $\frac{26-6}{2} = 10$, and 10 + 1 = 11. During these 11 days, the average distance she runs is $\frac{26+6}{2} = 16$ miles. So, her total distance is equal to 11 x 16 = 176 miles.

10. C: Let x be the number of pounds of large mushrooms. The price for any quantity is 6.95x. Two pounds of small mushrooms have a price of 2(5.95). For a quantity of the mixture, price equals 6.75(x + 2). This gives the equation 6.95x + 2(5.95) = 6.75(x + 2). To solve for x, use the distributive

165

property to multiply the terms on the right side. Then gather the variables on the left: 0.2x = 13.5 − 11.9 = 1.6, so that $x = \frac{1.6}{0.2} = 8$ pounds.

11. D: If R is the radius, then AB has length $2R$. Segment CB is also a radius and has length R. Since AC is tangential to the circle centered at point B, it must be perpendicular to the radius at point C. Therefore, ABC is a right triangle and, from the Pythagorean theorem, $AC^2 + CB^2 = AB^2$. Substituting R and rearranging yields $AC^2 = (2R)^2 − R^2 = 3R^2$. Solve for AC by taking the square root of both sides of this equation, which yields $AC = R\sqrt{3}$.

12. D: An irrational number is one that cannot be expressed as a simple fraction or as a ratio of integers. Since Choice A equals $\frac{17}{10}$, it is rational. Choice B, which equals 4, is also rational. However, Choice D is not, since $\sqrt{12} = \sqrt{3x4} = 2\sqrt{3}$, and $\sqrt{3} = 1.732050807569$ .... The number represented by the expression $\sqrt{3}$ involves an infinite number of digits after the decimal and cannot be resolved to a simple fraction.

13. B: The median of a set is the middle number. First, arrange the set so that its members are in order: {4, 9, 7, 12, 13, 14, 16, 45}. For a set with an odd number of members, the median would simply be the centermost numeral. For a set such as this one, with an even number of members, the median is the average of the two centermost numbers. These are 12 and 13, so the median is 12.5.

14. C: Attendance in 2004 decreased from about 12,000 to 10,000 visitors. In 2005 it rebounded to 15,000 visitors, an increase of 5,000. This is the greatest year-to-year increase shown on the chart.

15. D: The probability that the chosen number will match Jenny's at any single digit is 1:10, since there are ten numerals from 0–9, each with equal probability of being chosen. The probability that the entire number will match is the product of those probabilities. Since there are five digits, that is $\frac{1}{100,000}$.

16. C: First, find the least common denominator (LCD) for the numerator: $\frac{2+\frac{4}{y}}{\frac{y+2}{3}} = \frac{\frac{2y}{y}+\frac{4}{y}}{\frac{y+2}{3}}$. Next, simplify the numerator: $\frac{\frac{2y+4}{y}}{\frac{y+2}{3}}$. Next, rewrite the fraction as the product of the numerator and the reciprocal of the denominator: $\frac{2y+4}{y} \cdot \frac{3}{y+2}$. Simplify by factoring: $\frac{2(y+2)}{y} \cdot \frac{3}{y+2} = \frac{6}{y}$.

17. B: This is an application of the fundamental counting principle, which states that if there are x ways to do one thing, y ways to do another, and z ways to do a third, then there are xyz ways of doing all three, if order is important, and $xyz/(3x2x1)$ ways if order is not important. Regina has a choice of nine flavors for her first scoop. Since no flavor can be used twice, she has a choice of 8 remaining flavors for her second scoop. Similarly, she may choose among 7 flavors for the third scoop. Multiplying 7, 8, and 9 yields 504. However, since the order in which she chooses the three flavors is not important, 504 must be divided by the product of 3, 2, and 1 to account for the different orders that are counted using the previous equation. Thus, the total number of combinations is (9x8x7)/(3x2x1) = 84.

18. C: The triangles are similar because they have the same angles but different sizes. Congruent triangles have the same angles and are the same size. In an equilateral triangle, all three sides are the same length. Finally, in an isosceles triangle, two of the three sides are the same length.

19. C: Determine 15% of $30,000 and subtract it from the original price. Since 15% of $30,000 is $\frac{15}{100} \cdot 30,000 = 4,500$, this yields $30,000 – $4,500 = $25,500.

20. B: It takes 11 cuts to create 12 pieces, since the cuts are between the pieces rather than one cut per piece (just as it would take one cut to separate something into two pieces).

21. D: Let x be the number in question. From the problem description, write the equation $14 + 2x = 8$. Isolating the variable on one side of the equal sign yields $2x = 8 – 14 = –6$. Solving this equation for x yields $x = \frac{-6}{2} = -3$.

22. B: Imagine a line drawn from C to O. The angle COB is two times the measure of angle CAB, and is therefore equal to 40°. Therefore, angle COB subtends an arc segment equal to $\frac{40}{360} \cdot 720 = 80$ m.

23. A: At the point of intersection, the functions must be equal for the same value of x. To find this point, set the functions equal to one another and solve for x. The equality is expressed by: $-2x + 6 = 4x + 3$. Solve for x by isolating the variable-containing terms on one side of the equal sign. This yields $6x = 3$, or x = ½. To find the corresponding value of y, substitute this x-value into either of the original equations. For example, y= $4x + 3 = 4\left(\frac{1}{2}\right) + 3 = 2 + 3 = 5$. The point of intersection is (½, 5).

24. B: Since the seventh is a Monday, it follows that the 9th, two days later, will be a Wednesday. Subsequent Wednesdays will fall on 7 days, and multiples of 7 days, after the 9th, that is, $9 + n(7)$. Since $9 + 14 = 23$, B is correct. None of the other choices equals 9 plus a multiple of 7. Note that April 31st is not even a possibility since April has only 30 days.

25. D: Let Ken's rate of painting be the normal rate. That is, Ken gets 1 man-hour of painting done in an hour. Then the room requires 6 man-hours to be painted completely. Bob paints at a rate of $\frac{6}{4}$ = 1.5 man-hours of work per hour, since he can paint the room in 4 hours. If they work together, the overall rate of work will be 1 + 1.5 = 2.5 man-hours per hour, and the total amount of time required to paint the room will be $\frac{6}{2.5}$ = 2.4 hours. Since 0.4 hours = 24 minutes, this is 2 hours and 24 minutes.

26. B: Since the square is circumscribed, its side is twice the length of the radius, or $2r$, and its area is $4r^2$. The area of the circle is given by πr^2. The shaded area is the difference between these two, or $4r^2 - \pi r^2 = (4 - \pi)r^2$.

27. C: Each term T_n in the sequence is equal to the previous term plus the quantity $2(n – 1)$. For example, the third term equals $3 + 2(3 – 1) = 3 + 4 = 7$. It follows that the 6th term will equal 21 + $2(6 – 1) = 21 + 10 = 31$. Alternatively, you can see that you add 2 to the first term to get the 2nd, 4 to the 2nd term to get the 3rd, then 6, then 8. So, you would add 10 to the last term, which yields 31.

28. A: Since the interest rate is 4%, the amount paid after one year is $I = 0.04$ x P, where P is the amount of the original investment. Since I = $200, solving for P yields $P = \frac{200}{.04} = $5,000.

29. B: The slope of a straight line is the rate of change of the dependent variable (the y-variable) with respect to the independent variable (the x-variable). It is often described as the ratio of the *rise*, or change in y, to the *run*, or change in x. In this case, the y value increases from 2 to 8 (6 units) for a change in the x value from –1 to 3 (4 units). As a result, the slope is equal to the ratio $\frac{3}{2}$.

30. A: The pentagon may be considered the sum of a rectangle and a right triangle.

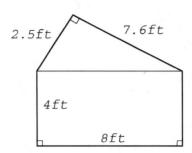

The area of a triangle is given by $A_T = \frac{1}{2}bh$, where b is the base and h the height. For a right triangle, one of the orthogonal sides may be taken as the height if the other is taken as the base. Thus, $A_T = \frac{1}{2}(7.6)(2.5) = 9.5$ square feet. The area of the rectangle is the product of its sides, $A_R = wl = 8(4) = 32$ square feet. The area of the pentagon is the sum of these, $A_P = A_R + A_T = 32 + 9.5 = 41.5$ square feet.

31. A: Let x represent the required number of cups of flour and set up the proportion $\frac{x}{8} = \frac{24}{50}$. Solving this proportion for x yields: $x = \frac{8(24)}{50} = \frac{192}{50} = 3.84$ cups of flour.

32. A: The area of $\triangle ABC$ is half of the area of the square. The area of the square is the product of base times height, or 10 x 10 = 100, so the area of $\triangle ABC$ is 50. To find the shaded region, we then must subtract the area of $\triangle BEF$. The area of a triangle is given by $A = \frac{1}{2}bh$, where b is the base and h is the height. Since $AE = EB$ and $BF = FC$, it follows that $EB = BF = 5$, this being one half the side AB. Thus, $A_{BEF} = \frac{1}{2}(5)(5) = 12.5$. Therefore, for the shaded region, $A = 50 – 12.5 = 37.5$.

33. C: Let k be the largest integer. Since they are consecutive and they add up to 36, we have the equation $k + (k - 1) + (k - 2) = 36$. Solving for k, we have $3k - 3 = 36$, or $3k = 39$, so $k = 13$. The consecutive integers adding up to 36 are 11, 12, and 13.

34. B: The length of the paper is 11 inches. Subtracting the two margins, the length of the printed picture will be 11 – 1½ – 1½ = 11 – 3 = 8 inches. Similarly, the width will be 8 ½ – 1½ – 1½ = 8½ – 3 = 5½ inches. The area of the picture is the product of length and width, or $A = 8(5.5) = 44$ square inches.

35. A: Let L_1 and W_1 be the length and width of rectangle I, and L_2 and W_2 the length and width of rectangle II. Then $L_1 = 1.5L_2$ and $W_1 = \frac{W_2}{1.5}$. The area of rectangle II is simply the product L_2W_2. The area of rectangle I is $L_1W_1 = 1.5L_2\left(\frac{W_2}{1.5}\right) = L_2W_2$. That is, the two areas are the same.

36. C: To determine this, you must solve the given equation for x. Since $10x + 2 = 7$, we have $x = \frac{7-2}{10} = \frac{5}{10} = 0.5$, and $2x = 1$. Alternately, $10x = 5$; divide both sides by 5 to get $2x = 1$.

37. B: If the first lap takes 50 seconds, the second one takes 20% more, or $T_2 = 1.2T_1 = 1.2(50) = 60$ seconds, where T_1 and T_2 are the times required for the first and second laps, respectively.

Similarly, $T_3 = 1.2T_2 = 1.2(60) = 72$ seconds, the time required for the third lap. Add the times for the three laps: $50 + 60 + 72 = 182$.

38. B: Zero is the only number that gives the same result when multiplied or divided by a factor.

39. D: All of the other capital letters shown are symmetrical with respect to a horizontal axis drawn through the middle as in the H shown in the figure. Only Z is not symmetrical in this respect.

40. B: The stock first increased by 10%, that is, by $10 (10% of $100) to $110 per share. Then, the price decreased by $11 (10% of $110) so that the sale price was $110 – $11 = $99 per share, and the sale price for 50 shares was 99×$50=$4950.

41. D: The sides of a triangle must all be greater than zero. The sum of the lengths of the two shorter sides must be greater than the length of the third side. Since we are looking for the minimum value of the perimeter, assume the longer of the two given sides, which is 6, is the longest side of the triangle. Then the third side must be greater than 6 – 4 = 2. Since we are told that the sides are all integral numbers, the last side must be 3 units in length. Thus, the minimum length for the perimeter is 4 + 6 + 3 = 13 units.

42. C: The hypotenuse is the longest side of a right triangle, so 6 and 8 are the legs. Calculate the length of the hypotenuse from the Pythagorean Theorem: $A^2 + B^2 = C^2$. Thus $6^2 + 8^2 = 36 + 64 = 100$. The square root of 100 is 10 and the perimeter equals 10 + 6 + 8 = 24.

43. A: The area of a triangle equals half the product of base times height. Since the base passes through the center, we have base = $2r$ and height = r, so the area A is $A = \frac{r(2r)}{2} = r^2$.

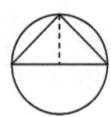

44. D: The probability of getting three aces in a row is the product of the probabilities for each draw. For the first ace, that is 4 in 52, since there are 4 aces in a deck of 52 cards. For the second, it is 3 in 51, since 3 aces and 51 cards remain; and for the third, it is 2 in 50. So the overall probability is $P = \frac{4}{52} \cdot \frac{3}{51} \cdot \frac{2}{50} = \frac{24}{132,600} = \frac{1}{5,525}$.

45. C: Since $70 represents 35% of Herbert's earnings, we can set up a ratio to determine what dollar amount corresponds to 15% of the earnings: $\frac{70}{35} = \frac{x}{15}$. Thus $x = \frac{70(15)}{35} = 30$.

46. C: She has been working at the rate of 10 papers per hour. She has 30 papers remaining and must grade them in the 2.5 hours that she has left, which corresponds to a rate of 12 papers per hour: $\frac{12}{10} = 120\%$ of her previous rate, or 20% faster.

47. D: The ratio of the ruler's height to the distance from eye to ruler must be the same as the ratio of the lighthouse's height to its distance. Since 2 feet is 24 inches, we have a ratio of $\frac{3}{24}$, which simplifies to $\frac{1}{8}$. So $\frac{1}{8} = \frac{60}{D}$ and $D = \frac{60(8)}{1} = 480$ feet.

48. A: The mean, or average of the distribution can be computed by multiplying each grade by the number of students obtaining it, summing, and dividing by the total number of students. Here, $n = 4.2$. The median is the value for which an equal number of students have received higher or lower grades. Here, $p = 4$. The mode is the most frequently obtained grade, and here, $q = 3$. Thus $n > p > q$.

49. D: 10% of the tested population of 40 students is 4 students. Four students got grades of 7 or higher.

50. A: Since a player cannot remove fewer than 1 or more than 3 toothpicks per turn, it follows that leaving 2, 3 or 4 toothpicks in a row allows a winning response, and that leaving 5 toothpicks forces the next player to leave 2, 3, or 4.

51. C: The line in the graph has a negative slope (because it moves downward from left to right) and a positive y-axis intercept (because it crosses the y-axis above the origin), so the factor multiplying the variable x, or the slope, must be negative, and the constant, or y-intercept, must be positive. The only answer choice that fits these criteria is C.

52. B: The volume of a rectangular prism can be determined by the formula $V = lwh$, or multiplying the length by the width by the height of the box. Therefore, the volume of the box described in this question is equal to 5 x 7 x 9, or 315 in³.

53. D: The circular area covered by the sprinkler is πr^2, so the two different areas can be calculated and subtracted: $\pi \cdot 8^2 - \pi \cdot 6^2 = \pi(64 - 36) = 28\pi \approx 88$ square feet.

54. C: Since the line is straight, the slope is the same throughout. Thus, if 5 x-units are traversed in going from $y = -3$ to $y = 0$ (where y increases from –5 to 0, to reach the origin), then 5 x-units will be traversed in going from $y = 0$ to $y = 3$.

55. B: Since there are equal numbers of each coin in the row, if two of one type are next to each other, two of the other type must also be next to each other someplace within the row, or else at each end of the row. Since the two dimes take up one end of the row, the two pennies must be together somewhere.

56. A: The median of a set of numbers is one for which the set contains an equal number of greater and lesser values. Besides Z, there are 8 numbers in the set, so that 4 must be greater and 4 lesser than Z. Arranging in order, the set is: {5, 7, 9, 12, Z, 16, 18, 23, 44}. So, Z must fall between 12 and 16.

57. C: If Q is divisible by both 7 and 2, it must be a multiple of 14, which is the least common multiple of both 2 and 7. Therefore, if one adds another multiple of 14 to Q, it will also be divisible by both 2 and 7. Of the choices given, only 28 is a multiple of 14.

Clerical Section

A great number of civil service positions are clerical in nature, and the exams usually reflect that by testing for clerical skills. The term "clerical" has the same root as the word "clerk," and employees who do these kinds of jobs used to be widely known as clerks. These days people tend to associate the term "clerk" with "cashier," and most people doing clerical work are now referred to as office workers, support staff, or some similar term. In most cases, a college degree is not required to be eligible for clerical positions. A high school diploma or general equivalency diploma will usually meet the educational requirement for applicants.

Clerical jobs can involve a wide variety of tasks. Some of the most common job duties for clerical workers are scheduling appointments, answering phones, keeping records, light bookkeeping, making copies, filing, sorting, word processing (what used to be called typing), and data entry. In many cases, one of these tasks will be the primary function of the employee. In other positions, a clerical worker will be more of a jack-of-all-trades, who may perform all of the tasks mentioned above on a regular basis, as well as others. Examples of clerical workers include secretaries and administrative assistants, who typically have a wide range of duties.

Until about 1980, most of these jobs were done the old-fashioned way, using pencil and paper, mimeographs, file cabinets, etc. Mimeographs are a thing of the past, of course, and while file cabinets, pencils, and paper are still found in offices, nearly all clerical work is now done with computers, printers, scanners, and other high-tech machines. In order to qualify for these jobs, you'll need to know at least the basics of operating a computer: working with documents, shortcuts like copying and pasting, saving files, etc. For some positions, you'll need extensive experience using common software programs for word processing, data management, creating charts, and more. If advanced skills are required, the civil service job listing will say so. Make sure to read job postings carefully so you don't waste time and expense, applying and testing for a job you aren't qualified for.

COMMON CLERICAL CIVIL SERVICE JOBS

FILE CLERKS

Keeping records is an important and time-consuming task in every government agency and department in the country. Without proper record keeping, it would be impossible for a government agency to properly serve the public, and it would be equally impossible for citizens to trust the agency. File clerks perform this vital function, and must do it accurately and efficiently. Some government departments are now paperless, meaning that all records and files are stored, updated, organized, and revised by electronic means only. In a paperless office, file clerks will do all of their work on computers. Most departments have not made the full transition to being paperless yet, however. In these jobs, much of the work will be done on computers, but since paper files are still in use, some of them will be stored in actual file cabinets. Some clerks may do only electronic filing or only paper filing, while some will do both.

INFORMATION CLERKS AND RECEPTIONISTS

There is a lot of overlap in the job descriptions of information clerks and receptionists, and oftentimes the titles are basically interchangeable. When you enter an office building and a person behind a desk greets and assists you, you're interacting with a receptionist. Generally speaking, receptionist jobs also involve answering phones and screening and directing calls. These activities take up most of a receptionist's day.

Information clerks often perform these same functions, but in many cases, they also interact with other employees, providing support in a variety of ways. They may look up needed information for a higher-level employee, for example. They may also do a fair amount of "gofer" tasks, which involve running errands or delivering work material from one employee to another. These employees tend to work with members of the public less often than receptionists do.

Since these two job titles are often used interchangeably, don't read too much into a job description on a civil service posting for a receptionist or information clerk position. If you qualify for one position, you'll probably qualify for the other, and the exams will almost certainly be very similar. The biggest difference between the two kinds of jobs is how much time an employee spends interacting with members of the public compared to the amount of time spent helping coworkers.

INFORMATION PROCESSING CLERKS

There are usually many jobs for information processing clerks in every government department. These positions fall into two main categories—word processing and data entry. Word processing used to be called typing, and being good at typing is still one of the main qualifications for these jobs. Both speed and accuracy are required; often the job listing will specify how fast an accurate you need to be in order to qualify. If so, you will need to pass a separate typing test. In addition, many of these positions require proficiency in Microsoft Word™, because it is the most common word processing software.

Data entry clerks work with numbers instead of words, and they may be referred to as accounting clerks or bookkeeping clerks. These employees use the numerical keypad on a regular keyboard, or a stand-alone device, known as a ten-key or a number pad (AKA numpad). Some jobs will require applicants to pass a test demonstrating that they have the necessary speed and accuracy on a ten-key pad.

CLERICAL PRACTICE TESTS

One thing all clerical positions have in common is that attention to detail is extremely important. Because of this, civil service exams for clerical positions have a lot of content designed to test for speed and accuracy at completing forms, coding, and spotting discrepancies between two sets of information. If you're considering applying for a clerical position, this section of the guide will help you get up to speed for this part of the civil service exam.

SECRET #1: SPEED

Practice at a higher rate of speed than your normal comfort level. This will increase your pace by the time of the exam. Your ability and tolerance for speed will increase after repeated practice. Remember to keep the accuracy ratio high. You must be fast but accurate.

SECRET #2: PREPARATION IS AN ADVANTAGE

Unlike others you will be prepared and know what is coming throughout the testing period. This should give you a level of comfort and confidence that will help you achieve a higher score.

SECRET #3: CHECK ANSWERS IF TIME ALLOWS

If you finish early, check your answers. Make sure that the answer for #4 is marked on the answer sheet as #4. Check any addresses that you were unsure of.

SECRET #4: DO NOT GUESS ON THIS SECTION

For most clerical exercises on a civil service exam, wrong answers will count against you in the scoring procedure. Your score will be reduced if you guess incorrectly instead of leaving a question blank.

FORMS COMPLETION
COMPLETING FORMS

This is a test of your ability to identify information needed to complete forms like those used by many delivery companies, which are similar to many departmental forms in government agencies. You will be shown several forms on this test, along with several items about what information is required to complete each form. Each part of the form is labeled (for example, 7 and 7a).

REDUCING ERRORS

Here are suggestions to help you reduce errors on Completing Tasks:

- Study each form carefully. Each of the forms in this test section is different and calls for different information in the various sections. You should take time to study the forms carefully before responding to the items to be sure that you know what information is desired.
- Consider answering items you're sure of, and then come back and answer other items later. If you return to an item, take extreme care to make sure that you are marking the correct answer on your answer sheet. It is easy to lose your place and darken the wrong circle.

FORMS COMPLETION SAMPLE QUESTIONS

Look at the sample form and questions shown below. Please study the form and complete the sample questions. Mark your answers in the *Sample Answer Grid*.

Sample Form

1. Last Name	2. First Name	
3. Street Address		
4. City	5. State	6. ZIP Code
7. Date 7a. Month 7b. Day 7c. Year	8. Amount Paid $	

S1. Where should the last name be entered on this form?

- A. Box 1
- B. Box 2
- C. Box 3
- D. Box 4

S2. Which of these is a correct entry for Line 7a?

   A. $62.30
   B. 2005
   C. August
   D. 70455

Sample Answer Grid	
S1.	Ⓐ Ⓑ Ⓒ Ⓓ
S2.	Ⓐ Ⓑ Ⓒ Ⓓ

Completed Sample Answer Grid	
S1.	● Ⓑ Ⓒ Ⓓ
S2.	Ⓐ Ⓑ ● Ⓓ

In the **Sample Form**, Box 1 is labeled "Last Name." Therefore, the correct answer is A. In the **Sample Form**, Line 7a asks for a month, and August is the only month among the answer choices. Therefore, C is the correct answer. Notice that the **Completed Sample Answer Grid** on the right side of the page shows the correct responses filled in.

Forms Completion Exercise

Give yourself 7 minutes to complete this exercise. While this test part is designed to allow sufficient time to read and review each form, it is important to practice responding to the items within a reasonable time period.

Read each form and answer the items based upon the information provided.

Sample Form 1

Attempted Delivery Notice	
1. Today's Date	3a. Sender's Name
2. Date Item(s) Sent	3b. Sender's Address
4. [] If checked, someone must be present at the time of delivery to sign for item(s)	
5. Enter number of each 5a. ____ Letter 5b. ____ Magazine/Catalog 5c. ____ Large envelope 5d. ____ Box	6. Postage 6a. [] If checked, there is postage due on the item(s) 6b. _____ Amount due
7. Delivery 7a. [] Item(s) will be redelivered tomorrow 7b. [] Please pick up the item(s) at your local Post Office. The item(s) will be available after: 7c. Date _____ 7d. Time _____	

1. Where would you enter the sender's address?

- A. Box 1
- B. Box 2
- C. Box 3a
- D. Box 3b

2. Which of these would be a correct entry for Box 2?

- A. A check mark
- B. 11/12/04
- C. 4
- D. Renae Smith

3. You could enter a date in each of the following boxes EXCEPT which?

- A. Box 1
- B. Box 2
- C. Line 5a
- D. Line 7c

4. Which of these would be a correct entry for Line 7d?

- A. PO Box 454 Robert, LA 70455
- B. A check mark
- C. 03/15/05
- D. 10:00 a.m.

5. Where would you indicate that the customer must pick up the item at the Post Office?

A. Box 43a
B. Box 5a
C. Box 6b
D. Box 7b

6. Which of these would be a correct entry for Box 3a?

A. Lydia Traylor
B. A check mark
C. 5453 Essen Lane Baton Rouge, LA 70809
D. $5.08

7. How would you indicate that there are two boxes to be delivered?

A. Enter "2" in Line 5a
B. Enter "2" in Line 5b
C. Enter "2" in Line 5c
D. Enter "2" in Line 5d

Sample Form 2

Mass Mailing Receipt	
1. Date	4. Name of Permit Holder
2. Post Office ZIP Code	5. Address of Permit Holder
3. 5-digit Permit Number	6. Telephone Number of Permit Holder
Blank	
7. Processing Category (check one)	8. Total Number of Pieces
7a. [] Letters	9. Total Weight
7b. [] Flats	9a. ___ pounds 9b. ___ ounces
7c. [] Automation Flats	10. 2-digit Cost Code
7d. [] Parcels	11. Total Paid
	$ _____

8. Luke Strait holds the mass mailing permit. Where would you indicate this?

A. Box 3
B. Box 4
C. Box 5
D. Box 6

9. Where would you indicate that 75,000 pieces were sent?

A. Box 3
B. Box 8
C. Line 7a
D. Line 10

10. How would you indicate that the processing category is "Automation Flats"?

A. Put a check mark in Box 7a
B. Put a check mark in Box 7b
C. Put a check mark in Box 7c
D. Put a check mark in Box 7d

11. **The total paid was $407.59. Where would you indicate this?**

    A. Box 6
    B. Line 9a
    C. Box 10
    D. Line 11

12. **Which of these would be a correct entry for Box 5?**

    A. 111 Lake Front Drive Miramar Beach FL 32550
    B. Berry Town Candies
    C. 2/10/04
    D. A check mark

13. **Which of these would be a correct entry for Box 10?**

    A. 30454
    B. 901-866-5243
    C. 30
    D. 70005-6320

14. **The Post Office ZIP Code is 77706. Where would you indicate this?**

    A. Box 1
    B. Box 2
    C. Box 3
    D. Box 9

15. **A number would be a correct entry for every box EXCEPT which?**

    A. Box 3
    B. Box 4
    C. Box 8
    D. Line 11

FORMS COMPLETION ANSWER KEY

1. D

2. B

3. C

4. D

5. D

6. A

7. D

8. B

9. B

10. C

11. D

12. A

13. C

14. B

15. B

CODING AND MEMORY

This practice test consists of two sections. The Coding section tests your ability to use codes quickly and accurately, using a coding guide for reference. The Memory section tests your ability to complete the same task, but without the benefit of referring to the coding guide. Instead, you must recall the coding guide from memory.

These tests usually follow the same format. In most cases, you will be shown a coding guide, along with several items that must be assigned a code. You must look up the correct code for each item and write your response on the answer sheet accurately and quickly. During the first section of the test part, you will be allowed to look at the coding guide while you assign codes. During the second section of the test part, you must assign codes based on your memory of the same coding guide. While the coding guide is visible, try to memorize as many of the codes as you can. These are the same codes that will be used in the memory section.

Note: During the actual test:

- You are not allowed to look at the codes when answering the items in the Memory section.
- You are not allowed to write down any addresses during the memorization period.

Memory for addresses questions are often considered one of the hardest parts of the exam. You will be given a set of boxes, each of which will contain addresses. After memorizing the content in the boxes, you will have to recall in which box each appeared.

SECRET #1: MEMORIZE HORIZONTALLY

Memorize the addresses horizontally, not vertically. This is more natural and will flow more easily for you.

SECRET #2: ANSWER THE QUESTIONS IN THIS SECTION IN ORDER

Answer all questions in order. Do not attempt to go through this section twice. There is not enough time for you to answer the ones that you think are easy and then attempt to go back and answer the others.

SECRET #3: SPEED

Practice at a higher rate of speed than your normal comfort level. This will increase your pace by the time of the exam. Your ability and tolerance for speed will increase after repeated practice. Remember to keep the accuracy ratio high. You must be fast but accurate.

SCORING ANSWERS

Typically, your score on this part of the civil service exam is based on the number of items that you answer correctly minus 1/3 of the number of items you answer incorrectly. In both sections of this test part, your score depends on how many items you can correctly assign a code in the time allowed. You may not be able to assign a code to all of the items before time runs out, but you should do your best to assign as many as you can with a high degree of accuracy. There is a penalty for guessing on this test. It won't be to your advantage to guess randomly. However, if you can see that one or more responses is clearly incorrect, it will generally be to your advantage to guess from among the remaining responses.

REDUCING ERRORS

On the test, you have several opportunities to work with the coding guide and practice memorizing the codes for each range of addresses before answering items on them based upon memory. Listen to the administrator's instructions. Do not become frustrated or discouraged; remain focused. Here are more suggestions to help you reduce errors on this portion of the test:

- Answer items you know and answer other items later. Remember that you have a time limit.
- As time permits, go back and attempt to answer the more difficult items. If you have narrowed a difficult item down to one or two choices, make an educated guess. If you return to an item, take care to make sure that you are marking the correct answer on your answer sheet. It is easy to lose your place and mark the wrong circle.
- Arbitrarily guessing will probably not help your score. If you can eliminate one or more of the answers, it may be to your advantage to guess.
- Work as quickly and accurately as possible. You are not expected to answer all items in the time allowed.
- Fully use the practice opportunities and memorization periods you are given to practice memorizing the codes.

COMPLETING EXERCISE: CODING

Move through items 1 through 15 and assign codes to each based upon the Coding Guide. Work as quickly and as accurately as possible.

Time yourself on this exercise. You should stop after 2 minutes. You may not be able to finish all of the items in this exercise in that time, but practicing with a time limit will give you a better feel for taking the actual test.

When you finish the exercise set, check your answers.

Exercise: Coding

CODING GUIDE	
Address Range	Delivery Route
1 – 99 Richoux Rd. 10 – 200 Hoffman Ave. 5 – 15 E 6th Street	A
100 – 200 Richoux Rd. 16 – 30 E 6th Street	B
10000 – 12000 Byers Lane. 1 – 10 Rural Route 1 201 – 1500 Hoffman Ave.	C
All mail that doesn't fall in one of the address ranges listed above	D
blank	Address	Delivery Route
1.	7 Richoux Rd.	A B C D
2.	102 Norwood Ave.	A B C D
3.	23 E 6th Street	A B C D
4.	16 E 6th Street	A B C D
5.	29 Richoux Rd.	A B C D
6.	8 Rural Route 1	A B C D
7.	1308 Hoffman Ave.	A B C D
8.	5 Rural Route 11	A B C D
9.	10191 Byers Lane	A B C D
10.	8 E 6th Street	A B C D
11.	183 Ridgeline Rd.	A B C D
12.	12050 Byers Lane	A B C D
13.	8 E 6th Street	A B C D
14.	1043 Hoffman Ave.	A B C D
15.	105 Richoux Rd.	A B C D
blank	blank	Blank

Coding: Answer Key

1. A

2. D

3. B

4. B

5. A

6. C

7. C

8. D

9. C

10. A

11. D

12. D

13. A

14. C

15. B

COMPLETING EXERCISE: MEMORY

In this section of the test, you will assign codes based on your memory of the Coding Guide. You will use the same Coding Guide you have been using throughout this exercise.

- Take 3 minutes to memorize the Coding Guide.
- You should not take any notes when memorizing the Coding Guide, but you may write in the test booklet while you are answering the items.
- Move through the items and assign codes to each based upon your memory of the Coding Guide. Do NOT refer to the Coding Guide as you work through this exercise. Work as quickly and as accurately as possible.
- You should not be able to see the Coding Guide during the exercise, and you should not turn back to an earlier page to look at it.
- Time yourself on this exercise. You should stop after 3 minutes. You may not be able to finish all of the items in this exercise in that time, but practicing with a time limit will give you a better feel for taking the actual test.
- When you finish the exercise, check your answers against the correct ones.

Exercise: Memory

blank	Address	Delivery Route
16.	12 E. 6th Street	A B C D
17.	1494 Hoffman Ave.	A B C D
18.	255 Richoux Rd.	A B C D
19.	165 Richoux Rd.	A B C D
20.	7 Rural Route 1	A B C D
21.	17 Rural Route 1	A B C D
22.	28 E 6th Street	A B C D
23.	14 E 6th Street	A B C D
24.	4500 Byers Lane	A B C D
25.	5 N 6th Street	A B C D
26.	39 Richoux Rd.	A B C D
27.	151 Richoux Rd.	A B C D
28.	8 E 6th Street	A B C D
29.	205 Hoffman Ave.	A B C D
30.	11001 Byers Lane	A B C D

Memory: Answer Key

16. A

17. C

18. D

19. B

20. C

21. D

22. B

23. A

24. D

25. D

26. A

27. B

28. A

29. C

30. C

How to Overcome Test Anxiety

Just the thought of taking a test is enough to make most people a little nervous. A test is an important event that can have a long-term impact on your future, so it's important to take it seriously and it's natural to feel anxious about performing well. But just because anxiety is normal, that doesn't mean that it's helpful in test taking, or that you should simply accept it as part of your life. Anxiety can have a variety of effects. These effects can be mild, like making you feel slightly nervous, or severe, like blocking your ability to focus or remember even a simple detail.

If you experience test anxiety—whether severe or mild—it's important to know how to beat it. To discover this, first you need to understand what causes test anxiety.

Causes of Test Anxiety

While we often think of anxiety as an uncontrollable emotional state, it can actually be caused by simple, practical things. One of the most common causes of test anxiety is that a person does not feel adequately prepared for their test. This feeling can be the result of many different issues such as poor study habits or lack of organization, but the most common culprit is time management. Starting to study too late, failing to organize your study time to cover all of the material, or being distracted while you study will mean that you're not well prepared for the test. This may lead to cramming the night before, which will cause you to be physically and mentally exhausted for the test. Poor time management also contributes to feelings of stress, fear, and hopelessness as you realize you are not well prepared but don't know what to do about it.

Other times, test anxiety is not related to your preparation for the test but comes from unresolved fear. This may be a past failure on a test, or poor performance on tests in general. It may come from comparing yourself to others who seem to be performing better or from the stress of living up to expectations. Anxiety may be driven by fears of the future—how failure on this test would affect your educational and career goals. These fears are often completely irrational, but they can still negatively impact your test performance.

> **Review Video: 3 Reasons You Have Test Anxiety**
> Visit mometrix.com/academy and enter code: 428468

185

Elements of Test Anxiety

As mentioned earlier, test anxiety is considered to be an emotional state, but it has physical and mental components as well. Sometimes you may not even realize that you are suffering from test anxiety until you notice the physical symptoms. These can include trembling hands, rapid heartbeat, sweating, nausea, and tense muscles. Extreme anxiety may lead to fainting or vomiting. Obviously, any of these symptoms can have a negative impact on testing. It is important to recognize them as soon as they begin to occur so that you can address the problem before it damages your performance.

> **Review Video: 3 Ways to Tell You Have Test Anxiety**
> Visit mometrix.com/academy and enter code: 927847

The mental components of test anxiety include trouble focusing and inability to remember learned information. During a test, your mind is on high alert, which can help you recall information and stay focused for an extended period of time. However, anxiety interferes with your mind's natural processes, causing you to blank out, even on the questions you know well. The strain of testing during anxiety makes it difficult to stay focused, especially on a test that may take several hours. Extreme anxiety can take a huge mental toll, making it difficult not only to recall test information but even to understand the test questions or pull your thoughts together.

> **Review Video: How Test Anxiety Affects Memory**
> Visit mometrix.com/academy and enter code: 609003

Effects of Test Anxiety

Test anxiety is like a disease—if left untreated, it will get progressively worse. Anxiety leads to poor performance, and this reinforces the feelings of fear and failure, which in turn lead to poor performances on subsequent tests. It can grow from a mild nervousness to a crippling condition. If allowed to progress, test anxiety can have a big impact on your schooling, and consequently on your future.

Test anxiety can spread to other parts of your life. Anxiety on tests can become anxiety in any stressful situation, and blanking on a test can turn into panicking in a job situation. But fortunately, you don't have to let anxiety rule your testing and determine your grades. There are a number of relatively simple steps you can take to move past anxiety and function normally on a test and in the rest of life.

> **Review Video: How Test Anxiety Impacts Your Grades**
> Visit mometrix.com/academy and enter code: 939819

Physical Steps for Beating Test Anxiety

While test anxiety is a serious problem, the good news is that it can be overcome. It doesn't have to control your ability to think and remember information. While it may take time, you can begin taking steps today to beat anxiety.

Just as your first hint that you may be struggling with anxiety comes from the physical symptoms, the first step to treating it is also physical. Rest is crucial for having a clear, strong mind. If you are tired, it is much easier to give in to anxiety. But if you establish good sleep habits, your body and mind will be ready to perform optimally, without the strain of exhaustion. Additionally, sleeping well helps you to retain information better, so you're more likely to recall the answers when you see the test questions.

Getting good sleep means more than going to bed on time. It's important to allow your brain time to relax. Take study breaks from time to time so it doesn't get overworked, and don't study right before bed. Take time to rest your mind before trying to rest your body, or you may find it difficult to fall asleep.

> **Review Video: The Importance of Sleep for Your Brain**
> Visit mometrix.com/academy and enter code: 319338

Along with sleep, other aspects of physical health are important in preparing for a test. Good nutrition is vital for good brain function. Sugary foods and drinks may give a burst of energy but this burst is followed by a crash, both physically and emotionally. Instead, fuel your body with protein and vitamin-rich foods.

Also, drink plenty of water. Dehydration can lead to headaches and exhaustion, especially if your brain is already under stress from the rigors of the test. Particularly if your test is a long one, drink water during the breaks. And if possible, take an energy-boosting snack to eat between sections.

> **Review Video: How Diet Can Affect your Mood**
> Visit mometrix.com/academy and enter code: 624317

Along with sleep and diet, a third important part of physical health is exercise. Maintaining a steady workout schedule is helpful, but even taking 5-minute study breaks to walk can help get your blood pumping faster and clear your head. Exercise also releases endorphins, which contribute to a positive feeling and can help combat test anxiety.

When you nurture your physical health, you are also contributing to your mental health. If your body is healthy, your mind is much more likely to be healthy as well. So take time to rest, nourish your body with healthy food and water, and get moving as much as possible. Taking these physical steps will make you stronger and more able to take the mental steps necessary to overcome test anxiety.

Mental Steps for Beating Test Anxiety

Working on the mental side of test anxiety can be more challenging, but as with the physical side, there are clear steps you can take to overcome it. As mentioned earlier, test anxiety often stems from lack of preparation, so the obvious solution is to prepare for the test. Effective studying may be the most important weapon you have for beating test anxiety, but you can and should employ several other mental tools to combat fear.

First, boost your confidence by reminding yourself of past success—tests or projects that you aced. If you're putting as much effort into preparing for this test as you did for those, there's no reason you should expect to fail here. Work hard to prepare; then trust your preparation.

Second, surround yourself with encouraging people. It can be helpful to find a study group, but be sure that the people you're around will encourage a positive attitude. If you spend time with others who are anxious or cynical, this will only contribute to your own anxiety. Look for others who are motivated to study hard from a desire to succeed, not from a fear of failure.

Third, reward yourself. A test is physically and mentally tiring, even without anxiety, and it can be helpful to have something to look forward to. Plan an activity following the test, regardless of the outcome, such as going to a movie or getting ice cream.

When you are taking the test, if you find yourself beginning to feel anxious, remind yourself that you know the material. Visualize successfully completing the test. Then take a few deep, relaxing breaths and return to it. Work through the questions carefully but with confidence, knowing that you are capable of succeeding.

Developing a healthy mental approach to test taking will also aid in other areas of life. Test anxiety affects more than just the actual test—it can be damaging to your mental health and even contribute to depression. It's important to beat test anxiety before it becomes a problem for more than testing.

> **Review Video: Test Anxiety and Depression**
> Visit mometrix.com/academy and enter code: 904704

Study Strategy

Being prepared for the test is necessary to combat anxiety, but what does being prepared look like? You may study for hours on end and still not feel prepared. What you need is a strategy for test prep. The next few pages outline our recommended steps to help you plan out and conquer the challenge of preparation.

STEP 1: SCOPE OUT THE TEST

Learn everything you can about the format (multiple choice, essay, etc.) and what will be on the test. Gather any study materials, course outlines, or sample exams that may be available. Not only will this help you to prepare, but knowing what to expect can help to alleviate test anxiety.

STEP 2: MAP OUT THE MATERIAL

Look through the textbook or study guide and make note of how many chapters or sections it has. Then divide these over the time you have. For example, if a book has 15 chapters and you have five days to study, you need to cover three chapters each day. Even better, if you have the time, leave an extra day at the end for overall review after you have gone through the material in depth.

If time is limited, you may need to prioritize the material. Look through it and make note of which sections you think you already have a good grasp on, and which need review. While you are studying, skim quickly through the familiar sections and take more time on the challenging parts. Write out your plan so you don't get lost as you go. Having a written plan also helps you feel more in control of the study, so anxiety is less likely to arise from feeling overwhelmed at the amount to cover.

STEP 3: GATHER YOUR TOOLS

Decide what study method works best for you. Do you prefer to highlight in the book as you study and then go back over the highlighted portions? Or do you type out notes of the important information? Or is it helpful to make flashcards that you can carry with you? Assemble the pens, index cards, highlighters, post-it notes, and any other materials you may need so you won't be distracted by getting up to find things while you study.

If you're having a hard time retaining the information or organizing your notes, experiment with different methods. For example, try color-coding by subject with colored pens, highlighters, or post-it notes. If you learn better by hearing, try recording yourself reading your notes so you can listen while in the car, working out, or simply sitting at your desk. Ask a friend to quiz you from your flashcards, or try teaching someone the material to solidify it in your mind.

STEP 4: CREATE YOUR ENVIRONMENT

It's important to avoid distractions while you study. This includes both the obvious distractions like visitors and the subtle distractions like an uncomfortable chair (or a too-comfortable couch that makes you want to fall asleep). Set up the best study environment possible: good lighting and a comfortable work area. If background music helps you focus, you may want to turn it on, but otherwise keep the room quiet. If you are using a computer to take notes, be sure you don't have any other windows open, especially applications like social media, games, or anything else that could distract you. Silence your phone and turn off notifications. Be sure to keep water close by so you stay hydrated while you study (but avoid unhealthy drinks and snacks).

Also, take into account the best time of day to study. Are you freshest first thing in the morning? Try to set aside some time then to work through the material. Is your mind clearer in the afternoon or evening? Schedule your study session then. Another method is to study at the same time of day that you will take the test, so that your brain gets used to working on the material at that time and will be ready to focus at test time.

STEP 5: STUDY!

Once you have done all the study preparation, it's time to settle into the actual studying. Sit down, take a few moments to settle your mind so you can focus, and begin to follow your study plan. Don't give in to distractions or let yourself procrastinate. This is your time to prepare so you'll be ready to fearlessly approach the test. Make the most of the time and stay focused.

Of course, you don't want to burn out. If you study too long you may find that you're not retaining the information very well. Take regular study breaks. For example, taking five minutes out of every hour to walk briskly, breathing deeply and swinging your arms, can help your mind stay fresh.

As you get to the end of each chapter or section, it's a good idea to do a quick review. Remind yourself of what you learned and work on any difficult parts. When you feel that you've mastered the material, move on to the next part. At the end of your study session, briefly skim through your notes again.

But while review is helpful, cramming last minute is NOT. If at all possible, work ahead so that you won't need to fit all your study into the last day. Cramming overloads your brain with more information than it can process and retain, and your tired mind may struggle to recall even previously learned information when it is overwhelmed with last-minute study. Also, the urgent nature of cramming and the stress placed on your brain contribute to anxiety. You'll be more likely to go to the test feeling unprepared and having trouble thinking clearly.

So, don't cram, and don't stay up late before the test, even just to review your notes at a leisurely pace. Your brain needs rest more than it needs to go over the information again. In fact, plan to finish your studies by noon or early afternoon the day before the test. Give your brain the rest of the day to relax or focus on other things, and get a good night's sleep. Then you will be fresh for the test and better able to recall what you've studied.

STEP 6: TAKE A PRACTICE TEST

Many courses offer sample tests, either online or in the study materials. This is an excellent resource to check whether you have mastered the material, as well as to prepare for the test format and environment.

Check the test format ahead of time: the number of questions, the type (multiple choice, free response, etc.), and the time limit. Then create a plan for working through them. For example, if you have 30 minutes to take a 60-question test, your limit is 30 seconds per question. Spend less time on the questions you know well so that you can take more time on the difficult ones.

If you have time to take several practice tests, take the first one open book, with no time limit. Work through the questions at your own pace and make sure you fully understand them. Gradually work up to taking a test under test conditions: sit at a desk with all study materials put away and set a timer. Pace yourself to make sure you finish the test with time to spare and go back to check your answers if you have time.

After each test, check your answers. On the questions you missed, be sure you understand why you missed them. Did you misread the question (tests can use tricky wording)? Did you forget the information? Or was it something you hadn't learned? Go back and study any shaky areas that the practice tests reveal.

Taking these tests not only helps with your grade, but also aids in combating test anxiety. If you're already used to the test conditions, you're less likely to worry about it, and working through tests until you're scoring well gives you a confidence boost. Go through the practice tests until you feel comfortable, and then you can go into the test knowing that you're ready for it.

Test Tips

On test day, you should be confident, knowing that you've prepared well and are ready to answer the questions. But aside from preparation, there are several test day strategies you can employ to maximize your performance.

First, as stated before, get a good night's sleep the night before the test (and for several nights before that, if possible). Go into the test with a fresh, alert mind rather than staying up late to study.

Try not to change too much about your normal routine on the day of the test. It's important to eat a nutritious breakfast, but if you normally don't eat breakfast at all, consider eating just a protein bar. If you're a coffee drinker, go ahead and have your normal coffee. Just make sure you time it so that the caffeine doesn't wear off right in the middle of your test. Avoid sugary beverages, and drink enough water to stay hydrated but not so much that you need a restroom break 10 minutes into the test. If your test isn't first thing in the morning, consider going for a walk or doing a light workout before the test to get your blood flowing.

Allow yourself enough time to get ready, and leave for the test with plenty of time to spare so you won't have the anxiety of scrambling to arrive in time. Another reason to be early is to select a good seat. It's helpful to sit away from doors and windows, which can be distracting. Find a good seat, get out your supplies, and settle your mind before the test begins.

When the test begins, start by going over the instructions carefully, even if you already know what to expect. Make sure you avoid any careless mistakes by following the directions.

Then begin working through the questions, pacing yourself as you've practiced. If you're not sure on an answer, don't spend too much time on it, and don't let it shake your confidence. Either skip it and come back later, or eliminate as many wrong answers as possible and guess among the remaining ones. Don't dwell on these questions as you continue—put them out of your mind and focus on what lies ahead.

Be sure to read all of the answer choices, even if you're sure the first one is the right answer. Sometimes you'll find a better one if you keep reading. But don't second-guess yourself if you do immediately know the answer. Your gut instinct is usually right. Don't let test anxiety rob you of the information you know.

If you have time at the end of the test (and if the test format allows), go back and review your answers. Be cautious about changing any, since your first instinct tends to be correct, but make sure you didn't misread any of the questions or accidentally mark the wrong answer choice. Look over any you skipped and make an educated guess.

At the end, leave the test feeling confident. You've done your best, so don't waste time worrying about your performance or wishing you could change anything. Instead, celebrate the successful

completion of this test. And finally, use this test to learn how to deal with anxiety even better next time.

Important Qualification

Not all anxiety is created equal. If your test anxiety is causing major issues in your life beyond the classroom or testing center, or if you are experiencing troubling physical symptoms related to your anxiety, it may be a sign of a serious physiological or psychological condition. If this sounds like your situation, we strongly encourage you to seek professional help.

How to Overcome Your Fear of Math

Not again. You're sitting in math class, look down at your test, and immediately start to panic. Your stomach is in knots, your heart is racing, and you break out in a cold sweat. You're staring at the paper, but everything looks like it's written in a foreign language. Even though you studied, you're blanking out on how to begin solving these problems.

Does this sound familiar? If so, then you're not alone! You may be like millions of other people who experience math anxiety. Anxiety about performing well in math is a common experience for students of all ages. In this article, we'll discuss what math anxiety is, common misconceptions about learning math, and tips and strategies for overcoming math anxiety.

What Is Math Anxiety?

Psychologist Mark H. Ashcraft explains math anxiety as a feeling of tension, apprehension, or fear that interferes with math performance. Having math anxiety negatively impacts people's beliefs about themselves and what they can achieve. It hinders achievement within the math classroom and affects the successful application of mathematics in the real world.

SYMPTOMS AND SIGNS OF MATH ANXIETY

To overcome math anxiety, you must recognize its symptoms. Becoming aware of the signs of math anxiety is the first step in addressing and resolving these fears.

NEGATIVE SELF-TALK

If you have math anxiety, you've most likely said at least one of these statements to yourself:

- "I hate math."
- "I'm not good at math."
- "I'm not a math person."

The way we speak to ourselves and think about ourselves matters. Our thoughts become our words, our words become our actions, and our actions become our habits. Thinking negatively about math creates a self-fulfilling prophecy. In other words, if you take an idea as a fact, then it will come true because your behaviors will align to match it.

AVOIDANCE

Some people who are fearful or anxious about math will tend to avoid it altogether. Avoidance can manifest in the following ways:

- Lack of engagement with math content
- Not completing homework and other assignments
- Not asking for help when needed
- Skipping class
- Avoiding math-related courses and activities

Avoidance is one of the most harmful impacts of math anxiety. If you steer clear of math at all costs, then you can't set yourself up for the success you deserve.

193

LACK OF MOTIVATION

Students with math anxiety may experience a lack of motivation. They may struggle to find the incentive to get engaged with what they view as a frightening subject. These students are often overwhelmed, making it difficult for them to complete or even start math assignments.

PROCRASTINATION

Another symptom of math anxiety is procrastination. Students may voluntarily delay or postpone their classwork and assignments, even if they know there will be a negative consequence for doing so. Additionally, they may choose to wait until the last minute to start projects and homework, even when they know they need more time to put forth their best effort.

PHYSIOLOGICAL REACTIONS

Many people with a fear of math experience physiological side effects. These may include an increase in heart rate, sweatiness, shakiness, nausea, and irregular breathing. These symptoms make it difficult to focus on the math content, causing the student even more stress and fear.

STRONG EMOTIONAL RESPONSES

Math anxiety also affects people on an emotional level. Responding to math content with strong emotions such as panic, anger, or despair can be a sign of math anxiety.

LOW TEST SCORES AND PERFORMANCE

Low achievement can be both a symptom and a cause of math anxiety. When someone does not take the steps needed to perform well on tests and assessments, they are less likely to pass. The more they perform poorly, the more they accept this poor performance as a fact that can't be changed.

FEELING ALONE

People who experience math anxiety feel like they are the only ones struggling, even if the math they are working on is challenging to many people. Feeling isolated in what they perceive as failure can trigger tension or nervousness.

FEELING OF PERMANENCY

Math anxiety can feel very permanent. You may assume that you are naturally bad at math and always will be. Viewing math as a natural ability rather than a skill that can be learned causes people to believe that nothing will help them improve. They take their current math abilities as fact and assume that they can't be changed. As a result, they give up, stop trying to improve, and avoid engaging with math altogether.

LACK OF CONFIDENCE

People with low self-confidence in math tend to feel awkward and incompetent when asked to solve a math problem. They don't feel comfortable taking chances or risks when problem-solving because they second-guess themselves and assume they are incorrect. They don't trust in their ability to learn the content and solve problems correctly.

PANIC

A general sense of unexplained panic is also a sign of math anxiety. You may feel a sudden sense of fear that triggers physical reactions, even when there is no apparent reason for such a response.

CAUSES OF MATH ANXIETY

Math anxiety can start at a young age and may have one or more underlying causes. Common causes of math anxiety include the following:

THE ATTITUDE OF PARENTS OR GUARDIANS

Parents often put pressure on their children to perform well in school. Although their intentions are usually good, this pressure can lead to anxiety, especially if the student is struggling with a subject or class.

Perhaps your parents or others in your life hold negative predispositions about math based on their own experiences. For instance, if your mother once claimed she was not good at math, then you might have incorrectly interpreted this as a predisposed trait that was passed down to you.

TEACHER INFLUENCE

Students often pick up on their teachers' attitudes about the content being taught. If a teacher is happy and excited about math, students are more likely to mirror these emotions. However, if a teacher lacks enthusiasm or genuine interest, then students are more inclined to disengage.

Teachers have a responsibility to cultivate a welcoming classroom culture that is accepting of mistakes. When teachers blame students for not understanding a concept, they create a hostile classroom environment where mistakes are not tolerated. This tension increases student stress and anxiety, creating conditions that are not conducive to inquiry and learning. Instead, when teachers normalize mistakes as a natural part of the problem-solving process, they give their students the freedom to explore and grapple with the math content. In such an environment, students feel comfortable taking chances because they are not afraid of being wrong.

Students need teachers that can help when they're having problems understanding difficult concepts. In doing so, educators may need to change how they teach the content. Since different people have unique learning styles, it's the job of the teacher to adapt to the needs of each student. Additionally, teachers should encourage students to explore alternate problem-solving strategies, even if it's not the preferred method of the educator.

FEAR OF BEING WRONG

Embarrassing situations can be traumatic, especially for young children and adolescents. These experiences can stay with people through their adult lives. Those with math anxiety may experience a fear of being wrong, especially in front of a group of peers. This fear can be paralyzing, interfering with the student's concentration and ability to focus on the problem at hand.

TIMED ASSESSMENTS

Timed assessments can help improve math fluency, but they often create unnecessary pressure for students to complete an unrealistic number of problems within a specified timeframe. Many studies have shown that timed assessments often result in increased levels of anxiety, reducing a student's overall competence and ability to problem-solve.

Debunking Math Myths

There are lots of myths about math that are related to the causes and development of math-related anxiety. Although these myths have been proven to be false, many people take them as fact. Let's go over a few of the most common myths about learning math.

MYTH: MEN ARE BETTER AT MATH THAN WOMEN

Math has a reputation for being a male-dominant subject, but this doesn't mean that men are inherently better at math than women. Many famous mathematical discoveries have been made by women. Katherine Johnson, Dame Mary Lucy Cartwright, and Marjorie Lee Brown are just a few of the many famous women mathematicians. Expecting to be good or bad at math because of your gender sets you up for stress and confusion. Math is a skill that can be learned, just like cooking or riding a bike.

MYTH: THERE IS ONLY ONE GOOD WAY TO SOLVE MATH PROBLEMS

There are many ways to get the correct answer when it comes to math. No two people have the same brain, so everyone takes a slightly different approach to problem-solving. Moreover, there isn't one way of problem-solving that's superior to another. Your way of working through a problem might differ from someone else's, and that is okay. Math can be a highly individualized process, so the best method for you should be the one that makes you feel the most comfortable and makes the most sense to you.

MYTH: MATH REQUIRES A GOOD MEMORY

For many years, mathematics was taught through memorization. However, learning in such a way hinders the development of critical thinking and conceptual understanding. These skill sets are much more valuable than basic memorization. For instance, you might be great at memorizing mathematical formulas, but if you don't understand what they mean, then you can't apply them to different scenarios in the real world. When a student is working from memory, they are limited in the strategies available to them to problem-solve. In other words, they assume there is only one correct way to do the math, which is the method they memorized. Having a variety of problem-solving options can help students figure out which method works best for them. Additionally, it provides students with a better understanding of how and why certain mathematical strategies work. While memorization can be helpful in some instances, it is not an absolute requirement for mathematicians.

MYTH: MATH IS NOT CREATIVE

Math requires imagination and intuition. Contrary to popular belief, it is a highly creative field. Mathematical creativity can help in developing new ways to think about and solve problems. Many people incorrectly assume that all things are either creative or analytical. However, this black-and-white view is limiting because the field of mathematics involves both creativity and logic.

MYTH: MATH ISN'T SUPPOSED TO BE FUN

Whoever told you that math isn't supposed to be fun is a liar. There are tons of math-based activities and games that foster friendly competition and engagement. Math is often best learned through play, and lots of mobile apps and computer games exemplify this.

Additionally, math can be an exceptionally collaborative and social experience. Studying or working through problems with a friend often makes the process a lot more fun. The excitement and satisfaction of solving a difficult problem with others is quite rewarding. Math can be fun if you look for ways to make it more collaborative and enjoyable.

MYTH: NOT EVERYONE IS CAPABLE OF LEARNING MATH

There's no such thing as a "math person." Although many people think that you're either good at math or you're not, this is simply not true. Everyone is capable of learning and applying mathematics. However, not everyone learns the same way. Since each person has a different learning style, the trick is to find the strategies and learning tools that work best for you. Some people learn best through hands-on experiences, and others find success through the use of visual aids. Others are auditory learners and learn best by hearing and listening. When people are overwhelmed or feel that math is too hard, it's often because they haven't found the learning strategy that works best for them.

MYTH: GOOD MATHEMATICIANS WORK QUICKLY AND NEVER MAKE MISTAKES

There is no prize for finishing first in math. It's not a race, and speed isn't a measure of your ability. Good mathematicians take their time to ensure their work is accurate. As you gain more experience and practice, you will naturally become faster and more confident.

Additionally, everyone makes mistakes, including good mathematicians. Mistakes are a normal part of the problem-solving process, and they're not a bad thing. The important thing is that we take the time to learn from our mistakes, understand where our misconceptions are, and move forward.

MYTH: YOU DON'T NEED MATH IN THE REAL WORLD

Our day-to-day lives are so infused with mathematical concepts that we often don't even realize when we're using math in the real world. In fact, most people tend to underestimate how much we do math in our everyday lives. It's involved in an enormous variety of daily activities such as shopping, baking, finances, and gardening, as well as in many careers, including architecture, nursing, design, and sales.

Tips and Strategies for Overcoming Math Anxiety

If your anxiety is getting in the way of your level of mathematical engagement, then there are lots of steps you can take. Check out the strategies below to start building confidence in math today.

FOCUS ON UNDERSTANDING, NOT MEMORIZATION

Don't drive yourself crazy trying to memorize every single formula or mathematical process. Instead, shift your attention to understanding concepts. Those who prioritize memorization over conceptual understanding tend to have lower achievement levels in math. Students who memorize may be able to complete some math, but they don't understand the process well enough to apply it to different situations. Memorization comes with time and practice, but it won't help alleviate math anxiety. On the other hand, conceptual understanding will give you the building blocks of knowledge you need to build up your confidence.

REPLACE NEGATIVE SELF-TALK WITH POSITIVE SELF-TALK

Start to notice how you think about yourself. Whenever you catch yourself thinking something negative, try replacing that thought with a positive affirmation. Instead of continuing the negative thought, pause to reframe the situation. For ideas on how to get started, take a look at the table below:

Instead of thinking...	Try thinking...
"I can't do this math." "I'm not a math person."	"I'm up for the challenge, and I'm training my brain in math."
"This problem is too hard."	"This problem is hard, so this might take some time and effort. I know I can do this."
"I give up."	"What strategies can help me solve this problem?"
"I made a mistake, so I'm not good at this."	"Everyone makes mistakes. Mistakes help me to grow and understand."
"I'll never be smart enough."	"I can figure this out, and I am smart enough."

PRACTICE MINDFULNESS

Practicing mindfulness and focusing on your breathing can help alleviate some of the physical symptoms of math anxiety. By taking deep breaths, you can remind your nervous system that you are not in immediate danger. Doing so will reduce your heart rate and help with any irregular breathing or shakiness. Taking the edge off of the physiological effects of anxiety will clear your mind, allowing your brain to focus its energy on problem-solving.

DO SOME MATH EVERY DAY

Think about learning math as if you were learning a foreign language. If you don't use it, you lose it. If you don't practice your math skills regularly, you'll have a harder time achieving comprehension and fluency. Set some amount of time aside each day, even if it's just for a few minutes, to practice. It might take some discipline to build a habit around this, but doing so will help increase your mathematical self-assurance.

USE ALL OF YOUR RESOURCES

Everyone has a different learning style, and there are plenty of resources out there to support all learners. When you get stuck on a math problem, think about the tools you have access to, and use them when applicable. Such resources may include flashcards, graphic organizers, study guides, interactive notebooks, and peer study groups. All of these are great tools to accommodate your individual learning style. Finding the tools and resources that work for your learning style will give you the confidence you need to succeed.

REALIZE THAT YOU AREN'T ALONE

Remind yourself that lots of other people struggle with math anxiety, including teachers, nurses, and even successful mathematicians. You aren't the only one who panics when faced with a new or challenging problem. It's probably much more common than you think. Realizing that you aren't alone in your experience can help put some distance between yourself and the emotions you feel about math. It also helps to normalize the anxiety and shift your perspective.

Ask Questions

If there's a concept you don't understand and you've tried everything you can, then it's okay to ask for help! You can always ask your teacher or professor for help. If you're not learning math in a traditional classroom, you may want to join a study group, work with a tutor, or talk to your friends. More often than not, you aren't the only one of your peers who needs clarity on a mathematical concept. Seeking understanding is a great way to increase self-confidence in math.

Remember That There's More Than One Way To Solve a Problem

Since everyone learns differently, it's best to focus on understanding a math problem with an approach that makes sense to you. If the way it's being taught is confusing to you, don't give up. Instead, work to understand the problem using a different technique. There's almost always more than one problem-solving method when it comes to math. Don't get stressed if one of them doesn't make sense to you. Instead, shift your focus to what does make sense. Chances are high that you know more than you think you do.

Visualization

Visualization is the process of creating images in your mind's eye. Picture yourself as a successful, confident mathematician. Think about how you would feel and how you would behave. What would your work area look like? How would you organize your belongings? The more you focus on something, the more likely you are to achieve it. Visualizing teaches your brain that you can achieve whatever it is that you want. Thinking about success in mathematics will lead to acting like a successful mathematician. This, in turn, leads to actual success.

Focus on the Easiest Problems First

To increase your confidence when working on a math test or assignment, try solving the easiest problems first. Doing so will remind you that you are successful in math and that you do have what it takes. This process will increase your belief in yourself, giving you the confidence you need to tackle more complex problems.

Find a Support Group

A study buddy, tutor, or peer group can go a long way in decreasing math-related anxiety. Such support systems offer lots of benefits, including a safe place to ask questions, additional practice with mathematical concepts, and an understanding of other problem-solving explanations that may work better for you. Equipping yourself with a support group is one of the fastest ways to eliminate math anxiety.

Reward Yourself for Working Hard

Recognize the amount of effort you're putting in to overcome your math anxiety. It's not an easy task, so you deserve acknowledgement. Surround yourself with people who will provide you with the positive reinforcement you deserve.

Remember, You Can Do This!

Conquering a fear of math can be challenging, but there are lots of strategies that can help you out. Your own beliefs about your mathematical capabilities can limit your potential. Working toward a growth mindset can have a tremendous impact on decreasing math-related anxiety and building confidence. By knowing the symptoms of math anxiety and recognizing common misconceptions about learning math, you can develop a plan to address your fear of math. Utilizing the strategies discussed can help you overcome this anxiety and build the confidence you need to succeed.

Tell Us Your Story

We at Mometrix would like to extend our heartfelt thanks to you for letting us be a part of your journey. It is an honor to serve people from all walks of life, people like you, who are committed to building the best future they can for themselves.

We know that each person's situation is unique. But we also know that, whether you are a young student or a mother of four, you care about working to make your own life and the lives of those around you better.

That's why we want to hear your story.

We want to know why you're taking this test. We want to know about the trials you've gone through to get here. And we want to know about the successes you've experienced after taking and passing your test.

In addition to your story, which can be an inspiration both to us and to others, we value your feedback. We want to know both what you loved about our book and what you think we can improve on.

The team at Mometrix would be absolutely thrilled to hear from you! So please, send us an email at tellusyourstory@mometrix.com or visit us at mometrix.com/tellusyourstory.php and let's stay in touch.